"Jason shares his life experiences with us in a way that inspires us to become a human being. His stories and reminders are not only interesting but motivating for our personal lives, teams and businesses."
- Howard Behar, Author of *It's Not About The Coffee* and Former President, **Starbucks Coffee**

"ReMembering is about optimizing our lives and focus in a distracting world. As always, Jason Barger inspires us to renew our vision and commitment to those around us. He shows us how our passionate leadership does change the world. I hope you'll join in and share this conversation with the memberships in your life."
- Brian Johnson, CEO of **en*theos** and creator of *PhilosophersNotes*

"Jason Barger is on to something very big here, and onto it with insight, grace and humor. Once again, he has found the heart of what drives us and can advance us as people, and then gives us the roadmap to get us there. ReMember is not just inspiring, it is also very useful, and Jason's work is a gift with meaning to us all."
- Douglas F. Kridler, President & CEO, **The Columbus Foundation**

BookRemember.com

ReMember

Renewing our memberships, relationships and focus in a distracting world

FIRST EDITION

© Copyright 2013

by Jason V. Barger

This book may be purchased for personal, educational, business, or sales promotional use. To obtain discounted bulk copies for your organization, please contact info@BookRemember.com. For other information please visit www.JasonVBarger.com or www.BookRemember.com

ISBN: 978-0-9910595-6-0

One Love Publishers

PRINTED IN THE UNITED STATES OF AMERICA

Cover Design: Adam Emery

ReMember

Renewing our Memberships Relationships Focus in a distracting world

By
Jason Barger

One Love Publishers

Dedicated to the family and friends who walk with me, support me, and remind me of the value of these messages. I'm especially grateful to the Tuesday morning group of guys who have contributed to my process to ReMember this past year. Thank you.

CONTENTS

Remember (verb)
: to keep an idea in your mind, to bring to attention again

ReMember (verb)
: to renew / recommit to your highest priorities, in mind and action

PREFACE

(The WHY of this book)

The world is changing. We know that. The question is, do we want to play any role in defining what it becomes?

I wrote this book because I know our actions contribute to defining the relationships, endeavors, and groups we belong to. This book is meant to begin a conversation as individuals and groups about what it means to come alive and engage.

I know it's easy for all of us to just go through the motions in life. You may be going through the motions at your job or on the team you work for every day. Others may be doing the same in their relationship with their spouse, significant other, kids, or friends. And many of us go through the motions with the traditional memberships and organizations we belong to.

The conversation I'm inviting you to participate in is about returning again in focus, spirit, and action to our highest priorities. It is a reminder about the impact we can have in the world. It's an invitation to come alive and play an active role in defining what those memberships become.

Thank you for joining in this conversation and sharing it with the important people in your life.

INTRODUCTION

(Where We've Been & Where We're Headed)

You may recall that the last time we crossed paths was either in a crowded airport terminal, or perhaps, just talking about airports. In 2008, I was the guy who quit his job and spent seven straight days flying to seven different cities — without leaving the airports the entire time. That profound journey was part of the creation of the book *Step Back from the Baggage Claim: Change the World, Start at the Airport.*

It came at a pivotal and vulnerable point in my life when I was stepping back and examining my life to determine the next steps along my path. The message of that book was the culmination of 10 beautiful years of serving others: building homes for the homeless, directing a large nonprofit summer camp for kids, and leading programs that encouraged us all to think about our core beliefs and the impact we have in the world. The book uses air travel as a metaphor to discuss the ways we travel through life. It is a passionate call to action to bring a spirit of patience, compassion, and generosity to air travel (and everyday life). In doing so, we can together impact the culture of the places we move in and out of. We can, one person at a time, name a new way to lead throughout the world. The Movement began (and it continues)!

I have been blown away by the response to the first book because I had no idea the metaphor of the baggage claim was going to resonate with so many people, be celebrated all around the globe, and lead to three other editions of the book: the Business Leader Edition (2010), the Healthcare Leader Edition (2011), and the Education Edition (2012). Since then I have been tremendously grateful to share the Step Back message with teams and organizations around the world. Across all sectors— business, healthcare, education, nonprofits, and communities of faith—a dialogue has begun about the kind of people, culture, and vision we have for the future. I have been blessed with the opportunity to give countless keynote speeches and workshops for groups. I founded Step Back Leadership Consulting LLC and now collaborate and partner with organizations to support the development of their people, shape their culture, and help them gain clarity on the mission and vision they have for the road ahead. It is amazing to see this spirit spreading and contributing in so many ways.

Stepping Back continues to be a powerful and contagious mindset for me and many others. Although it seems counterintuitive, Stepping Back is absolutely about how to move forward. But leadership development and culture change is not a "drive-through" experience; it doesn't happen overnight. Which is what has led us to this point. This book is about the thoughts, experiences, and lessons that have emerged over the last five years of this journey.

After we Step Back, the process of ReMembering is what moves us forward.

We've never lived in a more distracting, cluttered, and busy time than today. It's been said that we are bombarded by more than 3000 marketing messages every single day and that we shift our focus hundreds of times in a 12-hour day. It has never been harder (and more important) to stay focused on the things that matter most to us individually, to our team, or to our work in the world. This book is about what we choose to give our hearts, time, minds, and focus to every day. It's about coming alive and cutting through the distractions.

Remembering is such a common and necessary thing in our culture. We leave ourselves reminders about things we don't want to forget. We participate in ceremonies and rituals to remind us of that which is sacred to us. We celebrate the people and projects in our lives by remembering how and when they began.

But I want to invite us to think about the word remember slightly differently. In the pages to follow, you will learn more about what it means to ReMember in your life and work. We'll have a conversation about cutting through the distractions and entering into the proactive process of ReMembering—*renewing and strengthening the most important "memberships" in your life and work.* You'll discover what it means to:

6

1) **RePurpose:** — Return to the Mission
2) **ReLease:** — Let go of the baggage
3) **ReCast:** — Create a new vision for the future
4) **ReSpond:** — Put compelling action into motion
5) **Own It:** — Dare to live the life you want

We all have memberships. Formally, we belong to clubs, teams, organizations, associations, companies, churches, social networks, and brand loyalty programs, among other affiliations. More importantly, we also belong to our families, friends, communities, and our world. This book is about breaking out of the staleness of the status quo and renewing our memberships with passion, focus, and leadership. It is about the conscious choices we all make every day that create the lives we live. It is about coming alive — an awakening of sorts — and taking a more active ownership in the life we live and the groups, teams, and people we serve. A fast-changing world requires people — human beings — to work together and recommit to a vision to make anything happen. Membership isn't about merely "belonging." It is a choice about how we engage and where we contribute our gifts and strengths.

The very best leaders, teams, families, and organizations cut through the clutter and distractions of everyday life to bring their highest priorities to action in the world. I've realized in my daily life (that often contains many sticky note reminders of things I'm trying to remember), my effectiveness actually depends on focusing on a few key items I need to remember—and those become the ones that get my full attention. Engaging membership leads to powerful breakthroughs and connections. It's in the renewal process that we stimulate progress in all the areas of our personal lives and businesses, but is also the process that leads us to impact huge issues such as community building, poverty, social justice, disease, and caring for our environment. Engagement, passion, and authentic connections lead to solutions.

Just so you know from the beginning, the lessons in this book are written as much for me as they are for you. I want to share with you the processes I go through to take an authentic look at myself, what I think about, struggle with, and hope to be. Like you, I'm imperfect, but my goal is to live my life with gratitude, excellence, love, faith, and purpose. I come to this conversation with the root belief that we all play an active role in creating the lives and world we live in. Our actions are powerful and sometimes we need to remember why we do what we do, who we are trying to be, and how we want to move next.

Those who know me well know the mission I'm most compelled by in all of my work is what I refer to as the human element. One of the most common things I hear or observe when collaborating with organizations across all sectors is that the human element is what's missing most in the world today. In our rush to achieve, to score, to win, to maintain, to gain, to survive—whatever the pursuit— our humanity suffers. Yet the human element is the one we are in most control of. I know that my purpose (why I do what I do) is to inspire and encourage others to bring their gifts to serve the needs of the world. That is the compass for me and this journey.

Whether you are reading this book as a leader on your team at work, the parent of your family, a person of faith, a leader in your community, or all of the above, thank you for joining the conversation. Wherever you may be on your journey, I hope this book brings language, anecdotes, and questions that will help you and your memberships *thrive*! Remember, the memberships in our lives are not about a one-time transaction. They are enhanced by a continual process of renewal.

- Jason Barger

"What we see depends mainly on what we look for."
—Sir John Lubbock

<u>Chapter 1</u>

WHERE YOU LOOK IS WHERE YOU GO

I remember a friend describing the experience of learning to surf for the first time. He detailed the way the instructor taught the students to pop up on the board before they even left the sand.

"There is one main thing you all need to know first in order to learn to surf," the instructor began. "Where you look is where you go!"

As soon as you pop up on your surf board in the water, where you look is where you go. If you look down at the water out of fear, that's exactly where you're going. If your eyes look to your footing, you stumble.

The first thing you have to do is to put your eyes on where you want to go—the shoreline. Let your eyes steer where you go. It's a practice of focus, of attention, of vision.

I have been thinking an awful lot about surfing lately in my own life. We've never lived in a faster and more scattered time than we do today. Our eyes can be tricked into looking in so many different directions we become totally disoriented. Perhaps the 1980s philosopher Ferris Bueller was on to something when he reminded us, "Life moves pretty fast. If you don't stop and look around every once in a while, you could miss it." Well, I don't want to miss it. I don't want you to miss it. I think we have important contributions to make. We must keep our eyes focused on what matters most.

I'm Jason. I'm 38 years old. I have an amazing wife and three unbelievably cute, young, and active children. I have a tremendous family and friends who deserve quality time. I have my own business and vision for how I want to contribute to the world. I belong to groups, teams, and organizations that are important to me. I also probably have grass that needs to be mowed, emails filling my inbox, physical mail that "I'll get to soon," and demanding obligations of every sort. Like yours, my life is fast, full, wonderful, and complicated at times.

I'm certainly not perfect. I have my own doubts, fears, failures, worries, and hang-ups. I have a fairly clear vision of what success is supposed to look like in my career and as a father, husband, friend, and leader. There is a lot that I want to experience, accomplish, give, learn, try, and be. Every day I wake up with all of these desires converging and am left trying to decide how to spend my day.

In these moments, I need to remember. I need to take the time to remember what is most important in my life. I need to remember the purpose for how I choose to spend my time and efforts. I need to intentionally, clearly, and actively step back to move forward. Because, if I don't, I know that I can find myself rushing from place to place or scattered in a sea of commitments that don't get my best self. I know that I need daily practice that centers on where I focus—and what gets my attention.

I call this practice the process of ReMembering. ReMembering is looking at myself in the mirror, taking stock of my life, and in the present moment, deciding what to give my attention, focus, mind, and heart to. It is more about the road ahead than the road behind. It is also about giving my best to what I choose to commit to.

Because if I don't intentionally focus my eyes, it's way too easy to just "be busy."

Busy or effective?

You know the conversation. We all do it. It goes something like this:

"Hey, Jason, how's it going?" (It's always the same).

"Great, but really busy," I reply. "How are you?"

"Oh, me too. Super busy, but good" says my counterpart as he moves quickly down his path.

Sound familiar? Sit back sometime and listen to how many times we use the word "busy" in our everyday conversations. It has infiltrated everything we do. Okay, that might be a bit much, but you get my point. Somewhere along the line we have adopted "busy" as the most significant label we attach to our lives. We honor busyness. Some would say that we glorify busyness. We think it validates us. It's easy to hide behind, too. We really don't have to share anything significant if we just say we're busy. I'm not judging. I do it too.

I'm working to rid the word from my vocabulary. Because if I'm honest with myself, I don't think I'm too busy. True, my life is very full. As a husband, father of young kids, business owner, volunteer, and friend, I have a lot that I want to do, experience, and accomplish. But I think describing it as too "busy" might be a cop-out. The reality is that I/ we get distracted. In the midst of all I want to do, experience, and accomplish in life, I'm distracted by all the other things that are swirling around, not to mention the things that are beeping at me all day long and the messages coming in that are not urgent.

What you will read in the pages ahead are stories about my journey to cut through the distractions in my everyday life in order to be the best contributor I can be in the world. I have become convinced of the need to focus and to experience life intentionally. I have observed that the most productive, efficient, compelling, happy, faithful, and successful people in the world right now are the ones who are ReMembering—re-prioritizing their lives in the present moment.

ReMembering isn't about looking at the past; it's about focusing on all that we choose to give to the here and now. It's a process, a mindset, a reminder about when we're at our best as individuals, teams, families, organizations, and communities.

I remember walking the streets of downtown Seattle. I was in town for a keynote speech and, as I often do when I'm traveling, I left my hotel room to walk the streets of the city. It was a beautiful day in the Pacific Northwest. Gorgeous blue skies smothered the tall buildings and the streets were abuzz with activity. People were rushing in every direction. The steep streets of downtown Seattle and the view of the boats on the water provided a magnificent landscape.

As I made my way up one of the inclined streets with the mass of other bodies, out of the corner of my eye; I saw a large, fast-moving object come whipping around the corner. I jumped aside just in time to dodge it. I could feel the air sweep across my face as it passed me quickly. I have no idea how someone was not sideswiped by the racing bandit. I dusted myself off and swung my head around to see if I could get a look at the passing perpetrator.

It was a police officer riding a Segway! He was perched in an upright position on the vehicle, but his eyes were pointed directly down at his cell phone as he typed a text message and darted down the steep street. Once I (and everyone around me) was safe from his path, I chuckled about how even the people who are supposed to be telling us not to text and drive are just as distracted as we are. It was a hilarious, yet scary scene.

Not long after that encounter in Seattle, I was driving on a highway in another part of the country when I glanced over and noticed the driver in the car beside me reading a book while racing ahead at 72 miles per hour. An actual book! He had one hand on the steering wheel and the other was holding a hardbound book just slightly above the level of the steering wheel. His eyes bounced back and forth between the riveting novel and the road. Must have been a helluva book. I think it is safe to say that we are living in times that can be quite distracting and disorienting.

Hiss

My first September after college was spent backpacking in Europe with two of my college roommates. With very little in our bank accounts but adventure in our blood, we flew across the ocean. We were bound by nothing (or so it seemed) and carried our only possessions on our backs. Over the course of the month the three of us were together, we traveled from Stockholm, Sweden to Oslo, Norway, to Copenhagen, Denmark, to Prague, Czech Republic, through Austria, and down through parts of Italy, flying home from Rome. It was a month of exploring and living minimally, but maximizing the experience of life. It was a fabulous time.

Our trip, however, didn't get off to the greatest of starts (or give anyone much confidence in our directional wherewithal). After three wonderful days and nights exploring Stockholm, we were eager to take the rest of Europe by storm. We raced to the station to catch the next train to Oslo. Our packs were slung on our backs, and the whole world was ahead of us.

As we hurried to the station, we decided we better hit the bathroom before we boarded the train. We ran down one corridor in search of the bathroom. Nothing to be found. We raced down another corridor looking for signs. Searching very quickly, we saw the sign with two stick figures with a box around them with the word "Hiss" and an arrow pointing up the stairs. Fantastic! Our Swedish was elementary, but signs were universal. Just before racing up the flight of stairs, we heard the ding from an opening elevator and decided it was worth sparing our energy.

We shot out of the elevator on the top level. No bathroom was in sight and we rushed all the way to the end of the hall. By this point, we were all laughing and each one of us was pointing to the other one and blaming him for our directional challenges. We spotted another one of the signs that read "Hiss" but this time the arrow was pointing back down to the lower level. Where in the world did people go to the bathroom around here?

We quickly loaded back into the elevator and descended back to the first level. We again darted out in search of the most elusive bathroom in all of Europe. The sign pointed with an arrow down another hallway and we raced even faster than before. We were starting to get nervous about missing our train. The hallway came to an end and you guessed it—only another group of signs. With panting breaths and nervous giggles, we looked at the signs and tried to crack the code.

Finally the answer came. I can't truly recall which one of the sleuths solved the mystery, (although I'll take credit), but someone blurted out, "Hiss doesn't mean bathroom. It means elevator!" We were idiots, totally disoriented, and embarrassed that it took us three rides to figure it out.

That image stays with me today because I think the distracted and disorienting world we live in sometimes can feel like that search for the bathroom. In the chaos of family schedules, business meetings, or stressful deadlines, it's easy to lose our way. We can spend our entire days racing around "doing things" but accomplishing very little. We can be moving very quickly, but not even sure where we're going.

The waiting room

The receptionist couldn't have been more pleasant. He welcomed me to the building and directed me to the waiting room. "Thank you for coming, Mr. Barger," he said. "I'll give them a call to let them know you are here."

I took my seat on the couch. Five minutes passed. Then 10. At the 25-minute mark I began to think this might be a bit more than a "Sorry, but our meeting ran a little over." I approached the receptionist in a calm but inquisitive fashion. He assured me they knew I was here and he didn't know what the hold-up was.

I had not worked with this organization before, but I had had preliminary discussions with them about the leadership development and organizational culture work needed for their team. I had been recommended to them by another company, and they had already booked me for two future speeches. They are a very large organization and had called this meeting because in their words, "We need to get some things in place to help our dysfunctional team." They described the culture of their organization as a whirlwind, with people constantly going in different directions.

After I had waited 45 minutes, the two lead members of the team came around the corner and thanked me for being there. They were noticeably frazzled. Both were rubbing their eyes and clearly still occupied with whatever happened in the meeting they had come from.

A moment of awkward silence ensued as I waited patiently for them to look at me. There was a long pause.

"Okay, what are we here to discuss?" the woman began.

I glanced over at the man to see what his response would be. He, too, stared at me.

"Well, you called this meeting with me," I began slowly, but trying very hard to absorb the awkwardness of the moment. "You told me you had some items you wanted to discuss regarding the development of your team and culture and my upcoming speeches."

"*We* called this meeting?" she responded. In fact, she was the specific person who called me and set it up only weeks earlier.

It was a scene directly out of a *Saturday Night Live* sketch. I kept peeking over my shoulder to see if there were any hidden cameras or friends playing a funny trick on me. The next 20 minutes included my retracing the entire conversation we had already had weeks earlier and then asking them more questions about what they were trying to accomplish.

"I'm so sorry," they continued. "We're just so busy right now that I don't even know where to begin."

That's exactly what the workshops were supposed to be about. They clearly were needed. It took well over a year until someone else in the organization was ready (and able) to follow through on what they said they wanted. They were wonderful people, but moving way too quickly and not even sure how to stop. They were busy, but certainly not effective.

Over the past years of consulting with teams and organizations, I'm more convinced than ever of the importance of these simple questions: Where are we? Where are we going? Why? Who's doing what next? Organizations, large and small, get racing so quickly on *WHAT* they are trying to accomplish that they forget to step back and remember *WHY* and *HOW* they are planning to get there as a team. The most successful leaders, teams, and organizations are the ones that dedicate time to return to these important questions and creatively engage their people to commit to the vision and the journey.

In a business setting (but certainly not only in business), distractions are rampant. *The Harvard*

Business Review recently reported the results of a study called "The Multitasking Paradox." Using a software tool called RescueTime, the study authors recorded the number of times a worker shifted focus in an average day. They captured each time the worker moved from one task to another, one message to another, or one distraction to the next. The data painted "a sobering portrait of the frenetic modern worker, who switches tasks hundreds of times a day, on average (not including smartphone distractions)." One worker the study highlighted switched tasks 496 times in one day, which resulted in a mere 33 percent of productive work time that day. Instead of actually stimulating significant progress in his daily work, that worker was spending all day hopping from task to task—metaphorically pushing scattered pieces of paper around on his own desk.

In today's fast-paced, global economy and a world of instantaneous communication and technology, I can't tell you how many groups I've sat with where distractions are one of their biggest challenges. Every member of the team is going a hundred miles a minute with a thousand tasks they are trying to actualize. They get so sped up that often the most valuable exercise is to help them step back and enter into a process to remember why they came together as a team, where they are trying to go, and what leadership actions are going to get them there. It's a process of helping them identify their highest priorities and refocus on how they are going to accomplish them.

Messages come at us all day long from the people around us, on the radio and TV, in every store or restaurant we enter, and across the social platforms and websites we visit. We have phones beeping at us and information arriving through myriad pathways, all trying to capture our attention. It's not surprising we lose our way from time to time and need to remember where we are, why we're here, and what we're actually trying to accomplish.

Forbes Magazine, in collaboration with The Center for Creative Leadership, released an article last year about the pace we're running in our world and organizational lives. In the piece "Slow Down to

Speed Up" the authors highlighted how the very best teams and cultures are trying to slow down instead of increasing the pace of work. "That's right," the article said. "Slow down now and you will move faster, further and with greater purpose later—even when, or especially when, you are staring down the triple threat of complexity, speed, and uncertainty."

There may not be a more important thing we can do or more valuable way to spend our time than to sit with the people we work with—the people we rely on daily—and reconnect as a team. In the midst of the fast pace, we must be mindful of our purpose and mission; we must take the time to sift through the countless distractions or wasteful efforts.

The question I ask myself and invite the clients I work with to consider is this: Are you busy or effective? Are you filling your days with tasks that really aren't your highest priorities? Are you rushing around trying to cross off items on your task list that aren't critical to what you're trying to accomplish? Are you taking the path of least resistance or the path of your most important work?

The most effective leaders, teams, organizations, and families are the ones who are:

- Clear on the purpose of their efforts and what they are trying to create
- Disciplined enough to give their attention to the highest priorities first
- Relentless in identifying the actions needed next to bring their mission to life

Hard work and time are always part of the equation, but the trick is not to spend too much time chasing the items that aren't the most

> **effective** (adjective): adequate to accomplish a purpose, an intended result

important. The point is to eliminate busyness for the sake of busyness. We all have an infinite number of things we *could* do or ways to fill our time, but greater fulfillment and success come when we give our focus, attention, and best selves to the highest priorities at this moment.

Are you and the memberships in your life effective or just merely busy? The pages ahead will

lead you through a process of ReMembering—
returning to purpose, releasing that which holds you
back, casting a new vision for the future, and
responding with a bias toward action. Let's continue
this process of renewal.

Questions For Renewal

- *What is capturing your focus at this point in your life?*
- *Where in your life are you feeling "busy" and where are you "effective"? Why are you effective?*
- *How would you describe where you are right now in your personal life? Professionally?*
- *If you could only focus your attention on five things today, what would they be and how would you give them your attention?*

Bias Toward Action

Having a Bias Toward Action is not a bias toward busyness. It is about filtering through the clutter to identify the highest priorities today that need your attention. Then, put into motion with action. Use these three minutes of reflection for direct application.

Three minutes of reflection:
- Look at how you design your day. Are you blocking off time for specific centering, planning, and execution or are you bouncing from item to item in scattered fashion? Block off time that reflects your highest priorities today.

NOTES:

"Efforts and courage are not enough without purpose and direction." —John F. Kennedy

Chapter 2

REMIND ME WHAT THE POINT IS?

The first way to cut through distractions is to step back and remember purpose.

Your first Christmas as a married couple is special. Amy and I had been married on December 1, and it wasn't until we got back from our honeymoon that we set out to select our first Christmas tree. This was a very ceremonious event for a young couple.

Even though this was eleven years ago, I remember the evening as if it were yesterday. The wintry December air in Columbus, Ohio, caused small puffs of steam to billow with each breath. We drove around the city in search of a tree lot before finally steering our way into a church parking lot. It wasn't our church, but we figured that the Christmas trees they were selling were probably part of a fundraiser for something worthwhile. We figured this was as good as a spot as any to find our magical first tree.

It was a Saturday evening around five o'clock and as we walked up to the tree portion of the parking lot, we noticed that many people were making their way into the church for an evening mass. We approached an older man in his late fifties who appeared to be heading up this tree operation. His rosy red cheeks and the winter stocking cap hugging his ears told the story of this chilly evening. We stood there in the parking lot as he gave us the lay of the land and description of every cut of tree on the lot.

While we listened to his eloquent description of our options, we noticed a car that had pulled into the parking lot and was trying to get down the aisle to find an open spot to park. Our tree salesman was standing in the aisle way so the woman behind the wheel of the car waited ... anxiously ... annoyed ... but patiently for the man to move. Finally, she rolled down her window and said in a hurried voice, "Excuse me, Joe, may I please get by?" Amy and I had stepped out of the way, but the man operating the tree lot looked at the woman, took his time, and snapped as he slowly slid out of her way. "Sure, but you know mass starts at five o'clock," he barked. It was 5:06.

The car crept by in search of any open slot. The man went right back to his discussion with us as if nothing happened. Like deer in headlights, Amy and I stood still in the slightly awkward moment. But the moment was only getting started.

Joe's sharp tone had clearly upset the woman as she parked and popped quickly out of her car. The woman was on a mission (and you could see it on her face) as she marched directly up to him. Again, she called him by name and followed it with, "I don't appreciate you treating me that way as I'm trying to get to church."

"Well, you should have been here at five o'clock!" Joe responded with a firm voice.

Amy and I, the two deer, stood even more still, as we were completely caught off guard by this exchange. All we wanted was a magical first Christmas tree.

"I'm sorry, but I'm doing my best," the woman responded.

"Well, you should have been here at five o'clock!" Joe barked with an even louder tone.

"That is awful to say," the woman continued. "I'm trying my hardest, but with my recent divorce it isn't exactly the easiest thing to drop the kids off clear across town and get to church."

"Well, you should have been here at five o'clock!" he shouted again as the woman gave up the argument and rushed toward the church entrance.

Joe turned his attention back to us, rolling his eyes and shaking his head in disgust with the woman. He attempted to transition smoothly back into his sales pitch for the Christmas trees as if nothing had happened. After a few moments of silence, Amy and I said we were going to look elsewhere.

I choose to believe this was a nice guy who got caught up in a moment that didn't bring out the best in him. We all have our moments where we lose sight of the big picture and our emotions overtake us. But when our behavior is in obvious contrast to the purpose of the moment, perhaps we've lost our way. In the midst of our distractions or intense focus on the task at hand, we shouldn't forget what we're trying to accomplish. The irony of this man judging a woman for being late to church (while she's in the midst of a challenging divorce) and trying to sell Christmas trees at the same time was in complete contrast to the purpose of the church.

It was a sad reminder that we mustn't forget the big picture. We can't be standing in a church parking lot, selling Christmas trees as a fundraiser for the church, and at the same time yell at someone who's late for church for reasons we may not know. We must remember the purpose we're trying to accomplish. We have to take time to remember the point.

Under the bridge

Some of the most profound experiences of my life came from serving the homeless on the streets of my hometown, Columbus, Ohio. For the 10 years I worked at First Community Church, I was lucky to have the opportunity to dream up, develop, and lead projects that put service to others into practice. It was a tremendous privilege to mobilize people to meet real needs in the world and at the same time to help us all think about our own leadership, faith, and people we want to be. Our "Streets Mission" was one of those projects.

Every Thursday night, high school students, college students, and adults would come together to pack up warm meals and the most basic supplies, such as hats, gloves, blankets, and flashlights for those living on the streets. Our mission was simple:

1) Feed the hungry and clothe the cold

2) Share dignity and respect with everyone

3) Love one another

The relationships, trust, and care we established with those on the streets were deeply felt and life-changing for all involved.

The newspaper did a feature article on our project, and the next day my phone rang. The caller was one of the executives of a new luxury high-rise condominium building downtown. She had seen my name in the paper and decided to track me down.

From the first statement out of her mouth, I knew we weren't seeing our project's mission from the same perspective. Her message was that she was concerned by the number of homeless people who were living under the bridges in the area where this new luxury building was being developed. She was concerned that they would be an "eyesore" and would negatively influence the property value. She wanted me to stop our group from feeding them. She wanted them to go away. She thought we were the ones who were "keeping them homeless."

"How many people have you gotten off of the streets?" she demanded. I tried to explain to her that our mission was not to place *our* expectations on the lives of these people and to "get them off the streets" unless that was a choice they were making. I shared the three point of our simple mission with her.

She still didn't get it and wasn't happy. She was convinced I was the one who was making them homeless. I told her she was giving me *way* too much power and credit and talked to her about each person, by name, who was living in that area. I explained to her that they were homeless well before we showed up and would still be living under the bridge even if we stopped coming. I invited her to think about the possible role and partnership we could play together in serving the needs of the homeless and having a powerful effect on the community. She was very frustrated, and it was obvious that she wanted our mission to be about making these people disappear. We were at total opposite points of view. As the conversation reached a point where I recognized she was getting more and more frustrated and realized we needed to agree to disagree, I made the decision to encourage a partnership once again.

I invited her to consider making a donation to our project. The new development project would get wonderful press for contributing to the community and, in return, I would organize an initiative to help clean up the trash around the surrounding area. Both parties would win and it would be a positive collaboration to meet real needs. She declined and hung up.

That experience taught me two tremendous lessons:

1. Always know what your mission is.

2. Always make sure you understand *why* you are doing what you're doing.

When those challenging and confrontational questions came, I was glad I had clarity about our purpose and mission. There is no better use of time, education, or development than to make sure you and everyone on your team, in your family, or in your organization is clear on why you do what you do and what direction you're heading. Remember the point of what you're trying to accomplish.

Whether you see life through the lens of religious faith or not (hang with me), the point is applicable. The religions of the world all comprise ceremonies, stories, and practices aimed at helping us remember that which is sacred in our lives. Depending on which English translation of the Bible you read, the word *remember* shows up approximately 163 times. Jesus or one of the disciples always seemed to be saying, "Hey, remember this," as he went into a story or made a point. It's as if he knew we are wired to move so quickly and become distracted by all that is going on around us. He knew that we needed to stop and remember the main point. He knew we were going to have to practice this art of remembering because our lives are going to be full and it is easy to lose our way. So, for all of us: Hey, remember this!

Sultan

Last year I had the great honor to be asked to speak at the Global Leadership Conference for Entrepreneurs' Organization (EO). EO is a worldwide organization made up of entrepreneurs who founded or lead their own companies and have achieved an outstanding level of success. I was invited to speak about my book *Step Back from the Baggage Claim*, the attributes of 21st century leadership, and developing the teams within their companies. It is a fascinating group, and their annual global conference is an amazing collection of people from all around the world. Last year's conference happened to be in Manama, Bahrain, a small country in the Middle East near Iran, Iraq, and Qatar. I lived in Egypt for a year when I was in elementary school because my father was a global entrepreneur, so I was excited to get back to the Middle East and experience another country.

The day after my speech, I jumped into a taxi with a few of the EO members to go experience the city. We were told that we needed to see the Suque (city market) and the Al-Fateh Mosque, one of the largest mosques in the world, which can accommodate 7000 worshippers at a time. We hit the Suque and then made our way to the mosque.

As we walked up the front steps of the giant mosque, we were greeted by Sultan. Sultan was dressed in the traditional white robe and headdress, was wearing only black socks on his feet, and had a very impressive long, black, straggly beard. His smile was huge and his slightly heavy-set build fit his jolly persona perfectly. To be honest, his loving and jovial personality and spirit caught all of us off guard. He was unlike any image of a Muslim portrayed by the world media—and that was confirmed by both the Australian and Costa Rican who were with me.

For more than an hour, Sultan gave us a tour of this grand mosque and talked passionately about the history, rituals, and importance the mosque plays in the lives of Muslims. He explained the daily Islamic prayers (Fajr, Dhuhr, Asr, Maghrib, Isha) in great detail and chronicled how some are practiced at least 17 times a day. Yes, 17 times a day! We peppered him with questions about the words, the practice, and the commitment to these prayers. He responded gracefully to all of the questions and was excited to share. He concluded one of his descriptions of the prayers by saying that each prayer ends by the worshiper reciting the words "Peace be upon you, and God's blessing," once while facing the right, and once while facing left—an action to remind Muslims of the importance of others around them, both in the mosque and around the world. A pretty nice sentiment no matter what your background, faith, culture or tradition.

I'm convinced that if Sultan were the global poster boy for Islam, the perceptions of Muslims would be drastically improved around the world. His gentleness, care and spirit of a servant-leader were infectious. He was a joy to be with and he certainly got us all thinking.

Seventeen times a day?

My time with Sultan made me think about the dedication, focus, and purpose that guided so much of his everyday life. It caused me to think about my own life and question whether I pause enough times to remember the most important priorities and people in my life. I thought about how important that process of ReMembering really is and how powerful it is when it calls us out of the blur of distractions and into very clear and purposeful action.

Our conversation in the taxi leaving the mosque was equally fascinating. With a car full of entrepreneurs and business owners, each could not imagine how he would ever get anything done if he stopped 17 times a day. As one of the others stated, "Hell, I have a hard enough time getting to church once a week or attending our company leadership meeting once a month."

But was 17 times a day truly all that crazy? I started to just think about the math. For an average 16 hour day, this would mean pausing at the 57-minute mark of every hour. Call it prayer. Call it meditation. Call it a pause for perspective. Or, just call it a moment to refocus on the most critical tasks at hand. What if I did pause for a few minutes each hour? How would those three minutes of every hour impact my focus, presence, purpose, and effectiveness?

My brother, Mike, is one of my favorite people on planet Earth. (I just needed to get that in here). He works for Team Fishel, one of the finest utility construction and network installation companies in the United States. The company's history of developing "teammates" is inspiring. A couple of years ago, Team Fishel decided to take a look at the efficiency and effectiveness of its work crews—an example of how effective companies step back to assess their operations and identify how they can improve their mission.

One of the most valuable pieces of information that came out of the assessment was one of the simplest observations: The report concluded that if at the end of each day the job foreman took 24 minutes to gather with the team, quickly go over the plan for what they were going to do the next day, state what the goals were, and make sure they had all the tools necessary ready to go, productivity would increase by 5 percent. A 5 percent increase in productivity would lead to a 50 percent increase in profitability. That's right, a 50 percent increase by better using only 24 minutes each day!

What Team Fishel found was that this focused time helped them weed through the distractions, organize their tools better, and get the entire team on the same page. It was a few moments to remember what the goal was, what the next step of the mission looked like, and clarify how they were going to start again the next day. It allowed them to make a good company even better.

This story reminds me of what I refer to as the "purposeful break" phenomenon. Over that same 10-

year stretch of my career I mentioned earlier, I was honored to lead more than 1700 people to construct 125 houses for families living in poverty in Mexico and the Dominican Republic. Some of the most profound moments of my life have come while working alongside others in the dirt to build a house for a family in need. It was truly a privilege to do the work. In addition to building the houses, the entire experience was designed to help the participants think about their own lives, develop their own leadership, and think about what it means to live out their faith and core values every day.

Each year as I prepared the leadership team for huge expeditions that included anywhere from 150 to 214 participants, I talked to the foremen of each building team about the importance of "purposeful breaks." I implored them, at some point halfway through each day of building, to stop everything they were doing, put down their tools and gather their entire team together. I encouraged them sit on the ground in a circle and take a rest, while at the same time asking two questions of the group: 1)

"How do you feel about what we're doing?" and 2) "What do you think we ought to do next?" Then I suggested they get out of the way and let the conversation happen.

Slowly, team members would begin to share why they even chose to come on this trip, what they were feeling about the family we were building the house for, and why they were determined to do the job well. For 20 to 30 minutes, the group dived into the purpose of the work. For a brief time they stepped back from the minutiae and details of the long workday and connected to the big picture of their mission. They took time to ReMember—to reinvest in their personal and team goals. Then they went back to work renewed.

Every single year, as I explained this concept to the team leaders before the trip, I would get the same response. Without fail, there was always a group that was skeptical. Typically, they were successful leaders or managers in their companies, and they challenged the idea this was a good use of our time. They thought it was grossly inefficient.

Entrenched in the building plans, they already had anxiety about how they were going to possibly get everything accomplished in the amount of time we had. They knew they had to delegate and race in order to finish on time. They were so focused on the tasks that the mission was secondary. They were buying into the myth that "the faster we run the further we get." Believe me, now that I'm working with groups around the world, I know the belief in this myth is alive and well — but absolutely not true.

Calmly, I would say to them, "Just please trust me." Some did. Some didn't. In the end, the teams whose leaders bought into the purposeful break philosophy had a dramatic outcome. Almost every year my group finished our project a good couple of hours to a half-day ahead of the others. And I'll tell you this with all sincerity, it had nothing to do with my construction abilities. I was functional, but not an expert by any stretch of the imagination. I am certainly no Bob the Builder, Ty Pennington, or Handy Manny.

I'm convinced it was because of the intentional time we took every single day to realign to the mission and the feelings of the team, and to let them participate in the choices about the actions that were needed next. The two questions: 1) "How do you feel about what we're doing?" and 2) "What do you think we ought to do next?"—engaged the group in ways that pure delegation could not. The energy of the team coming out of each of these purposeful breaks was palpable.

We were clearer about the next actions needed, who was going to own which piece of it, and what our next set of goals or benchmarks were. Most importantly, the group was more firmly rooted in the purpose of our mission. Every single time, it was amazing to watch individuals and the collective team come alive with more passion and focus than before. We were re-energized by the purpose of our mission and clear on our next highest priorities on the journey. All from taking a few minutes to remember.

Our memberships

As I said at the beginning of this book, ReMembering isn't just a moment of looking backward at our past, but is a process that moves us forward. It is looking at ourselves in the mirror, taking stock of our lives, and in the present moment, deciding what to give our attention, focus, mind, and heart to.

All of us have memberships. I mentioned the myriad examples of the kinds of memberships we belong to in the introduction of this book. I believe all of these memberships involve an element of choice. No, I did not choose the family I grew up in (although I got damn lucky), I do believe there is an active choice that I make to be a part of that family today. Whether I realize it or not, I am making an active choice each day to be a contributing member to the groups I care about. I make choices all day long about how I am going to contribute to my membership in marriage, my family, my friendships, and other groups.

Similarly, I have made a choice to do the work I do. I am a member of my own company. I have made a choice to partner with other companies and organizations to help support, serve, and assist in developing the leadership of their members. Even though I became an official member of my church more than 20 years ago, I am still making an active choice to be a member today. When I volunteer for an organization or serve on a board, I am making an active choice to support their mission.

The memberships (relationships) to which we give our time, resources, minds, and hearts are what make up our lives. We are a collection of the memberships we choose to honor. And because of where I am in life right now, I realize that these memberships are

renew (verb): to make new, fresh or strong again

not just a one-time commitment, but require a periodic renewal of the commitments. After 11 years of marriage, Amy and I need to go through the process of renewing our membership. As our oldest child, Will, turns 9, we need to go through the process of renewing our membership as parents. When I reached the 12-month mile marker with a company I'm helping with leadership development, culture, and vision, we needed to renew our membership. We did not simply renew my *contract* to consult; we took time to step back to remember the mission and renewed our *commitment* to move forward together. When we commit to renew our memberships, it's always a good thing. Re-up, Renew, ReMember.

Plato once wrote, "What is honored will be cultivated." Whatever we choose to honor each day with our focus, time, money, devotion, and heart is what will be cultivated in our lives. If we honor busyness, distractions, and chasing things that are not our highest priorities, that is the life that gets cultivated. But if we honor a purposeful, loving, positive, grateful life, and our actions are rooted in our highest priorities, we cultivate a different kind of life.

Why we exist

It's never a wasted effort to remember why we exist. Anyone experiencing hyper-growth in the business world, or is part of a high-octane culture focused on results knows how easy it is to get racing in many scattered directions. Somebody has to remember to check the compass. Somebody has to help remind the group *why* they exist in the first place. If not, it's easy to get way off track.

James Collins and Jerry Porras, in their highly acclaimed business book *Built To Last*, share words from a speech given by David Packard to his staff at Hewlett-Packard (HP) during a critical time in its existence.

"I want to discuss *why* (emphasis his) a company exists in the first place. In other words, why are we here? I think many people assume, wrongly, that a company exists simply to make money. While this is an important result of a company's existence, we have to go deeper and find the real reasons for our being. As we investigate this, we inevitably come to the conclusion that a group of people get together and exist as an institution that we call a company so that they are able to accomplish something collectively that they could not accomplish separately— they make a contribution to society, a phrase which sounds trite but is fundamental."

In the midst of our many memberships, the first step is to take time to remember the purpose for which they exist and why we joined. Then, we must go through the vital process of ReMembering—why, how, and in what ways we will recommit to our most important memberships. The rest of this book is about the critical process we choose when we ReMember (renew our memberships). Every successful individual, team, and organization on the planet, whether they realize it or not) goes through this process. It starts with remembering their mission and purpose and then moves into the process of recommitting to the journey ahead —

- **ReLease:** — Let go of your baggage
- **ReCast:** — Create a new vision for the future
- **ReSpond:** — Put compelling actions into motion
- **Own It:** — Dare to live the life you want

Join me on the next leg of this journey of renewal.

Questions For Renewal

- *What's your "WHY"? If you had to write a purpose statement for your life and work, what would it say?*

- *Are there memberships, relationships or specific projects in your life that have gotten off track and missing the purpose?*

- *What is the Mission of your team, your family, your business?*

- *When do you take time for purposeful breaks for you personally and with the key people in your life and work?*

Bias Toward Action (Not Busyness)
Three minutes of reflection:
- Which "membership" in your life and work needs your attention today? Make time to think about or discuss the two questions: How do you feel about what you're doing? What do you think you ought to do next?

NOTES:

"When I let go of what I am; I become what I might be."

—Lao Tzu

Chapter 3

LET GO OF THE NESTLE´ CRUNCH BAR

It was a defining moment. At seven years of age, I stood facing nearly my entire Indian Guides tribe. Indian Guides, a father / son camping activity that grew out of the YMCA organization of the 70's was a staple for young kids and dads in our town. However, I do remember the day I finally realized that Indian Guides was really just an excuse for the dads to take the kids camping and have a cold beer in the woods. Really quite brilliant. The boys who were in our tribe growing up are now dads themselves and spread all across America, but I hold a special place for them in my memories of childhood. Something significant always seemed to happen on one of our campouts.

So there I was face to face with my fellow Indian Guides. My Indian Guide name was "Firefox". Why, you ask? Well, because I was seven years old and it sounded super cool and tough to me.

The dads were still back at the dinner table of the country restaurant where we stopped on our way home from our latest camping excursion. As usual, the boys were running wild and up to no good. We dashed off to the arcade near the lobby of the restaurant.

"Firefox, I bet you can't get one of those candy bars," one of the other Indian Guides dared. We were standing right next to a giant candy bar vending machine. Through the glass you could see every pretty candy bar right in a row, taunting us. I wasn't about to back down from a challenge.

"Bet I can," I replied.

"Then do it!" they chanted. The rest of the Indians were circling.

"I will," I said boldly.

"Come on! Don't be scared," they pushed.

This was a defining moment. Either I was going to define it or it was going to define me. I looked down at my long pencil-thin arm and the opening at the bottom of the machine where the candy drops out. I was sizing up how far I thought I could reach and which of the coveted candy bars I would grab. Victory was certainly going to be a special kind of sweet.

A hush came upon the group of seven-year old boys as Firefox made the courageous first move. The metal door squeaked of old age as I pushed it open and began slithering my arm up toward the prize. The other Indians couldn't believe I was doing it. I could see they were a bit nervous to lose this bet.

My arm crept higher and higher into the mouth of the machine.

All of a sudden, pain struck me like the bite from a coiled viper. The anti-theft device installed on the inside of the machine (and certainly out of view or comprehension of a seven-year-old) clamped down on my small hand. The pain shot down my arm as I panicked and tried to wiggle free from the device. My body was now smashed against the outside of the machine and my arm was all the way up inside. Tears welled in my eyes as I fought away the pain and tried to hide my agony from anyone.

My loyal and wonderful Indian braves, as soon as they saw I was stuck and had tears in my eyes, scattered. Literally, every ally I had in the world ran for safety. I was now all alone with no tribe around me, and it was hard to hide the kid with his arm jammed up the candy machine. Finally, a man at the checkout register paying his bill turned around and saw me wrestling the machine. I was losing.

"Son, are you okay?" he asked with bewilderment. (Somehow he had never seen this before.)

I shot him the "Of course I'm not fine" look you give a man while you're being assaulted by a vending machine. I couldn't fight back the tears any longer and they streamed from my eyes. When the table of dads were notified, they jumped up as if they had just been told the place was on fire. The ambulance was already on its way.

Apparently, to get a boy's hand out from a candy bar machine, you need the "Jaws of Life," — the giant metal device used to cut people out of cars after a serious accident. The first responders had to cut that machine in half to locate my hand and pry it loose.

After a totally unrecognizable amount of time, I was finally freed from the tyranny of the evil machine. My hand was throbbing, and the medics told me that if it had been two inches higher in the machine I might have lost it. To this day I'm not sure if that was just a scare tactic from the medics or if it truly was a possible result from this street fight for a Nestle´ Crunch.

As my dad lovingly put his arm around me (he never once got mad at me and already knew that I understood what I had done was stupid) and we began to walk out the exit, the manager of the restaurant came over and handed me a candy bar. With a renewed sense of energy, I twirled around and stared directly at my fellow Indian Guides. With the candy bar raised in the air, I declared victory!

It was a defining moment and I defined it. Right? Or, perhaps the lesson is that sometimes you need to just know when to let go.

Monkey traps

I remember seeing a show on TV once about how people caught monkeys somewhere clear on the other side of the globe from where I live. The host of the show detailed how the trappers would find trees that had fallen on the ground, hollow out the middle portion of the tree, and put a little piece of food inside the log. Then, on the top part of the trunk on the outside of the log, they would drill a small hole right above where the food was. That was it.

As monkeys swung around the jungle, they would catch a whiff of the food and come exploring. Their noses would lead them directly to the hole on the top side of the fallen tree, and I imagine their eyes expanded at the sight of the beautiful treat down inside the hole. A monkey would wiggle its hand down through the narrow hole until it could grasp the food. But as it clinched its fist around the food, its hand was now too big to pull back through the hole.

The monkey would stand on top of the log struggling, pulling, and fighting to get the treat out of the log. Persistent and determined to capture the prize, it would fight and struggle without letting the food out of its clasp. The trappers would then come along and put the monkey into a net or cage and off they would go. Easy as that.

The monkey wasn't willing or never realized that all it had to do was let go of the food, unclench its fist, and then slide its hand back out of the hole. All it had to do was let go in order to be free.

The reason I share this image is not only to compare myself to a monkey with my attempt at liberating the candy bar. The reason those two images resonate so profoundly with me is because I see us all getting stuck in the ruts of life from time to time. I watch us all fall into the patterns of routine, what's comfortable, or what we know. We build walls of stability around ourselves that sometimes trap us right where we are. We hold onto something so tightly that it keeps us from moving anywhere.

The other thing that keeps us in the ruts of everyday life is our fear and doubt about what is possible. We can become so paralyzed by our fears or doubts about the future that they trap us right where we are. Like the monkey with its hand stuck in the hole, we need to let go in order to be free. We can't find something new until we're ready to release what's holding us back.

I believe a significant step in the process of ReMembering, of renewing our memberships, is releasing the baggage, burdens, and stresses of the past. In *Step Back from the Baggage Claim*, I talk about how we never truly know the baggage others carry beneath the surface of their lives. The fact is that every single one of us has baggage. We all have things in our lives that have not gone the way we hoped they would.

With groups I work with, I talk about the three different kinds of baggage we carry:

> **baggage** (noun): intangible feelings, circumstances, or beliefs that get in the way, weigh us down

Events, Consequences, and Thoughts. Events are the things that happen to us. Things that are out of our control: the weather, the economy, disease, accidents, betrayal from someone, and a whole range of other eventualities. We then carry the baggage, the burden, and the stress from how that event negatively (or sometimes even positively) affected our life. We struggle to make sense of it, it becomes a weight that we carry.

Consequences are the types of baggage that come from a cause and effect relationship we've played a role in. Something that we did, said, or worked on, that didn't play out the way we had hoped. An action (or non-action) we contributed to a situation that played a role in changing the outcome. There is baggage we carry then as we try to figure out how to move on, work through it, rebound, salvage it, or not repeat it.

Perhaps the most significant kind of baggage of all is our Thoughts. As the famous motivational speaker Zig Ziglar once said, "The most influential person you will talk to all day is yourself ... be careful what you say." The stories we tell ourselves and the way we make sense of the world, how we perceive it, and how we choose to respond, creates our reality. So many of us spend way too much time carrying around the baggage of the stories we tell ourselves — the negative thoughts that consume us — and the tragedy is that most of them are false. We can't let our doubts, fears, or false stories weigh us down and render us incapable of moving forward. We must be able to name and be honest about the baggage we carry and identify two things:

1) What is the baggage we can't do anything about (and might not even be true) and actively choose to let go of?

2) What is the baggage we can't let go of but need to learn to carry in a healthier way?

Can we make the choice to let go—to release the baggage?

The Biggest Loser

My wife, Amy, was very into the TV show *The Biggest Loser* for a few years. She didn't miss an episode. She was emotionally invested and cheering on the contestants. At first, I didn't know much about the show and kind of mocked her about being so involved. From a distance, I wasn't all that interested in a show called *The Biggest Loser* and didn't want to watch a show that highlighted people who were struggling through life. On the surface, it seemed like a total waste of time and exploitation of these people.

Well, she broke me down by her insistent urging until I finally watched an episode with her. I was caught between that tricky place in all marriages —trying to partake in something she was excited about even when I had little to no interest. As usually happens, she won out. She's very good.

For those of you who have been living on Planet Krypton for the last few years, *The Biggest Loser* involves a number of contestants who are significantly overweight and whose health is in jeopardy. Over the course of the show the contestants work with professional trainers to see who can lose the most weight, get to a healthier place in life, and win a cash prize. About one episode in, I saw exactly what was so compelling to Amy.

Not only is it inspiring to watch people who have so far to go work and work and work to lose every inch, but a pivotal point also comes in each of their journeys. There is a point of clarity each of them reaches about something in their past that they have been holding onto. It usually centers around an Event that happened to them, a consequence of a situation that didn't go their way, or a tragically debilitating story that they've been telling themselves for years about their own self-worth, limitations and capabilities, and life. It is at that exact moment when they can name the baggage that has turned into physical weight on their bodies that the television show ceases being about a contest and becomes rooted in the magnificent journey of someone's life.

When they make the very difficult decision to release that baggage, to let go of the burdens from their past, they take the first real step toward new life. It is compelling and it does bring tears to your eyes. Only then can they truly move forward.

Author Neale Donald Walsh once said, "You cannot let go of anything if you cannot notice that you are holding it. Admit your 'weaknesses' and watch them morph into your greatest strengths."

Part of renewing the memberships in our lives is releasing the baggage of our past (or getting clarity on how to better carry the baggage as we walk into the future). Recognizing what we're holding onto, what is weighing us down, our doubts, our fears, and then letting them go, is unbelievably liberating. It's what enables us to go forward. When we make that powerful choice to release what weighs us down, we're able to become something new. It happens to us individually in our personal lives for sure, but also collectively as groups and organizations.

Burberry

For more than a century, Burberry has been one of the most iconic brands in luxury fashion—a historic winner over the long haul. But, when Angela Ahrendts took over as CEO in 2006, she knew things needed to change, and quickly. She assessed the current state of the company and surveyed the market to see how other luxury competitors such as Louis Vuitton and Pinault-Printemps-Redoute (PPR) were doing in the economy of that time. Burberry was inching along at a two percent growth rate per year, a sign of aging for a brand like this. She had to do something.

Her assessment was that the company had way too many designers designing way too many items in a distracted and scattered manner. Burberry needed to let go of old modes of operation to move into new life. To propel the company forward, she knew she would have to make some hard decisions about letting people go. She had to release some baggage of past structures and gain greater clarity and focus regarding the company's scattered efforts.

Within one year, Burberry let the entire Hong Kong design team go, closed its New Jersey factory and its popular Welsh factory. Ahrendts took enormous heat from longtime company employees and those who knew their rich history well. But she knew the company had to let go of the weight that was keeping it from operating at full potential. Part of the company's remembering process was to reconnect to its core mission and purpose.

It's played out very well for Burberry. In Ahrendts' own words, "We've doubled the head count at Castleford since then and almost tripled our global workforce to nearly 10,000, adding more than 1,000 jobs in the UK over the past two years alone."

Ahrendts and Burberry are one of the many examples of teams and organizations that made the bold move to filter through the diversions of the modern world, release their baggage, and actively choose to renew their memberships. The famous mythologist and author Joseph Campbell once wrote, "We must be willing to let go of the life that we've planned, so as to have the life that is waiting for us." Our mental blocks about the way we've imagined our lives, our careers, our families, and our world are often what keep us from fully living the life that is right before us. When we drop the baggage of our fears, our doubts, the lives we've imagined, or "the way we've always done it," we are liberated to move into a world of new possibilities. The most authentic and courageous leaders and organizations actively challenge the status quo, put down their baggage and, in doing so, are free to envision their future and respond with compelling action.

Life after Favre

The saga went on for years. It was a ritual in the sports world that every February through August we would spend time discussing the lingering football question: when would legendary quarterback Brett Favre retire from the Green Bay Packers? It was the perfect storm for media curiosity and banter: an iconic football franchise and the modern-day face of the franchise, its soon to be Hall of Fame quarterback. The owners were trying to discern when it was time to change the course and move into the future.

Radio talk shows would light up with callers dying to give their points of view. Many were appalled at even the suggestion that the Packers would consider life after Brett Favre. After all, he *was* the Green Bay Packers. He had won a Super Bowl. He was their identity. Without him, they would cease to be relevant.

Others knew the Packers history was larger than one player. They knew and celebrated the unbelievable run that Favre had at the helm, but they also knew it couldn't last forever. They knew they couldn't hijack the entire future of the franchise because of an unwillingness to let go of the past.

Finally, after years of speculation, in 2008 the Green Bay Packers made the decision to hand the reins over to quarterback Aaron Rogers, who had been Favre's backup for three years. With tears, scars, and an abundance of uncertainty, the team let go of Brett Favre and attempted to make room for their future. There were plenty of skeptics for how this was going to turn out.

The result was surprising to many. In 2008, his first year as the starter, Rogers led the Packers to a 6-10 record, but showed tremendous promise for the future by passing for more than 4,000 yards and 28 touchdowns. In 2009, he helped turn the Packers from a six-win team to an 11-win team. In 2010, Aaron Rogers hoisted the Vince Lombardi Super Bowl trophy for the Green Bay Packers and was honored as the Super Bowl XLV Most Valuable Player.

One of the toughest things we do in life is let go of that which has been great for us in the past. Not only do we hold onto negative baggage about things that didn't go the way we wanted in the past, but we also hold on to positive baggage or memories from the past. We sometimes can hold onto our past successes so tightly that we're paralyzed. We can't step into the future. It's important to always remember, honor, and celebrate the success of the past, but to not let it define us in the present. Every so often it is time for us to release our hold on the past to make room for what we may become. There always comes a time when we need to trust and have faith that there is more good awaiting us and be reminded of our resources within.

The Golden Buddha

Brian Johnson is a friend and also happens to be the creator of Philosophers Notes, the En*theos Academy for Optimal Living, among others. He also introduced me to the documentary *Finding Joe*, in which he plays a role. This fantastic film is centered on the life of Joseph Campbell, author, mythologist and teacher, and the journey toward self-discovery. It beautifully weaves in the perspectives of many different people who have set out on the journey to "follow their bliss" in life. It's engaging, stimulating, and powerful.

Finding Joe references an old Buddhist story about the Golden Buddha. The quick version of the story goes a little like this. Many, many years ago in a village in Thailand stood the Temple of the Golden Buddha. A huge Buddha statue made of pure gold stood outside the monastery. Day after day, people came to the statue for meditation, prayer, and silence. It was a very treasured part of the village.

One day, word came that a nearby army had plans to attack their village. Many were worried that the invading troops would steal or harm the Golden Buddha, so they came up with a very clever idea. The villagers covered the Golden Buddha with mud and concrete so it would look like a normal stone statue and thus hide its true beauty and value.

The plan worked brilliantly. As the troops made their way toward the monastery, they raced right past the statue as if it were worthless. The fighting went on for years and slowly even the people within the village who had covered the statue in the first place forgot about the Golden Buddha. Even they saw it as an old concrete statue. Many years later, a monk sat down at the base of the statue for his daily mediation. As he rose from his seat, a piece of rubble crumbled beneath him. A chunk of the concrete had fallen off the statue and revealed a shiny piece of gold. The monk ran into the village with shouts of joy about the gold that was beneath the surface. The villagers joined together to chip away the outer shell of the concrete and unearth the Golden Buddha.

This metaphor reminds us that we are all born of great value. But over time and through the trials, tribulations, conformity, and distractions of life, we often build up a hard outer shell. We protect ourselves and can forget how truly valuable we really are inside. We begin to think we're the concrete

81

rather than the beautiful gold. Eventually, at critical moments in our lives, we actively choose to let go of what is hiding our best selves and rediscover the gold within.

As the Buddha reminded us, "In the end, only three things matter. How much you loved, how gently you lived, and how gracefully you let go of things not meant for you."

Complex relationships

While on a recent out of town trip, I had breakfast with an acquaintance I had not seen in years. He is not a close friend of mine and I didn't know much about the happenings in his life. He shared with me he was going through the final stages of a divorce. I knew very little of his situation, but listened as he described the last five years of their relationship, which included many lies, distrust, excessive alcohol, and two people committed to two different directions in life. They worked diligently for years with marriage counseling to try to rectify the pain and distrust, and develop a common vision for the life they could create together. Finally, it became abundantly clear that they weren't willing to make the kind of adjustments necessary to move their marriage into a healthy partnership.

As we sat across from each other at breakfast, he wasn't looking for my advice, but it was obvious he was looking for my acknowledgement and thoughts on the path ahead. He spoke about the difficulty of wrestling with his own beliefs about honoring the "institution" of marriage, but being stuck in a relationship where both parties were unwilling to honor the same things. When you boiled it right down, they were not both 100 percent committed to making it work—to designing a positive, loving relationship.

I explained to him that I usually don't advocate for divorce, but I also don't advocate for honoring a relationship in which each person is not willing to honor him or herself. If a piece of paper is all that is keeping them married, then I advocate for compelling conversation and personal ownership of a shared vision or separate visions (depending on what they decide) for the direction of their lives. I advocate for taking the time as a couple to Step Back and remember the words from their wedding day. To enter into the conversation about ReMembering and the new agreement they are willing to work toward.

But in this case, it was clear they could not make a new agreement; the relationship had come to its end and needed to be released. For both of their sakes, they needed to put down their baggage and open themselves to the more compelling lives each was committed to creating.

As he spoke with passion about the road ahead, I could see the excitement in his eyes. He talked about the contributions he wanted to make in the world, the vision for the healthier life he desired to lead, and the actions he was willing to hold himself accountable for to make it a reality. This was not the way he imagined his life going, so he knew he had to let go to move forward. He was liberated. He could now begin rebuilding the positive, healthy life he imagined. (And, by the way, so could she.)

The relationships we have in our lives can be quite complex. We all have burdens, baggage, and stresses which weigh on us. Being honest about the baggage is the beginning of the conversation about how to move more positively into the future. We have to be committed to the hard work that follows. (For those looking for good conversation starters, see the back of the book for suggestions).

We all have memberships that can be enhanced by our willingness to let go of past happenings or mental constructs. We all also may have complex memberships that have become too heavy to carry and are unhealthy. Some memberships have lived their purpose (or don't live out your true purpose), and are now ready to be released. We can't continue to add commitments or memberships in our lives without real clarity on what we're willing to let go of. It's in that process of letting go that we make room for the memberships we're ready to build. Only when we let go can we make room for what's next.

What do you need to let go of? What are you holding onto too tightly? What must you release to move ahead? How will you recognize, celebrate, honor, and remember the gold within yourself and others around you? If we cannot recommit to a membership, it is time to let it go. When we are ready to let go of the Events, Consequences or Thoughts that weigh us down, we are ready to move forward into a new reality. We are ready for new growth, new possibilities, new clarity, new challenges, new hope.

Questions For Renewal

- *Is there an Event, Consequence or Thought in your life currently or from your past that you are holding onto too tightly?*

- *What is the baggage you are carrying in your family? On your team? Within the business or organization you serve?*

- *Is there a "this is how we've always done it" you need to let go of?*

- *What is the Gold (strengths, beauty, capabilities) that is within you (and others in your life and work) that needs to be rediscovered?*

Bias Toward Action (Not Busyness)

Three minutes of reflection:

- What is a burden that is weighing on you day after day? Name it and identify what elements are things you can't do anything about and what you just need to carry in a healthier way. What one to three commitments will you make to yourself to move forward?

NOTES:

"When we change the way we look at things, the things we look at change." —Wayne Dyer

CHAPTER 4

PUT ON YOUR NEW EYES

Halftime shows at sporting events sure have taken a big step forward in the last decade. It seems like at almost every football or basketball game of note these days has a contest where a fan has a chance to win thousands of dollars. Whether it's a half-court shot for free college tuition or throwing a football at a target for cash, it's a fun and participatory communal event for the entire stadium.

I remember watching a college football game this last bowl season where Dr. Pepper was giving the winner of the contest a handsome amount of money. Two contestants, both men in their early twenties, had thirty seconds to throw as many footballs as they could through a cardboard hole in a target about twenty yards away. As they got in their stance and carefully watched for the timer to start, it was obvious that both men had spent weeks practicing their throws. The guy on the left looked to be about six feet two inches tall and even had the look of a quarterback. The guy to the right was much shorter and appeared to be your typical average Joe.

As the clock ticked and the crowd cheered, the guy on the left—the one with the look of a quarterback—grabbed the balls one at a time. He wound up with the textbook form of an NFL quarterback, and spiraled the balls at the target. He was very accurate. Throw after throw was precise, quick, and beautiful. Every handicapper in Vegas would have had this guy pegged as the clear favorite based solely on the "look test."

However, the average Joe-looking guy on the right was not even standing the way you are supposed to throw a football. In fact, he was crouched over the bucket of footballs with his chest facing straight at the target. He scooped the balls up at a much quicker pace and shoveled them like a basketball chest pass toward the target. It was an amazing and surprising sight to see.

When the buzzer went off and the crowd screamed, the average Joe-guy had more than doubled the number of balls thrown on target compared to his competitor. It was a colossal upset. In this contest, the conventional technique was clearly not the most effective approach.

I personally experienced this phenomenon at a child's birthday not too long ago at a local Chuck E. Cheese's. As the party was coming to an end, one of the other dads tapped me on the shoulder, showed me the few game tokens still left in his hand, and pointed at the Pop-o-Shot basketball game—the game where competitors have one minute to shoot as many miniature basketballs into the small basket as possible. The baskets were right next to one other so we each got to play directly against each other in real time. The challenge was on.

Being a former high school and college basketball player, his was a good kind of challenge for me. We made our way over to the Pop-o-Shot games and immediately started letting the balls fly. I had my technique down. I was barely even looking at the balls as I scooped them up and fired with precision and accuracy. I could feel my friend next to me shooting and I knew I was teaching him a lesson. We each frantically tossed up our last shots right as the buzzer went off. It was a blowout. I took him by a good twenty points.

The congratulations began from my friend and the onlookers who had wandered over from the party. There was a spattering of comments from the crowd about my playing days and praise for my basketball prowess. Just at the height of my enjoyment of this tasty victory and growth of my ego, we heard the sounds of the scoreboard exploding from the Pop-o-Shot game directly next to us.

A 15-year-old kid who was at least six inches shorter than I, and with his pants hanging down below his bum, was lighting it up. We watched in amazement, mesmerized by his style. He didn't even bother shooting the shots like a basketball shot. He grabbed the balls underhand and flicked them with his wrist up off the backboard as quickly as he could grab the balls. There was no semblance of the form I had been taught my whole life at basketball camps or from coaches from pee-wee leagues through college. Suddenly, nobody was all that impressed with me.

The fatal mistake made by each of the losers of the Dr. Pepper football throw contest and the Pop-o-Shot challenge was that we saw the games only as we knew them to be. We thought that for a football-throwing contest, you had to be able to throw the football with textbook form. We all knew cognitively how we were taught to throw a football. For Pop-o-Shot, we figured that the best basketball player would be the one who knew how to best shoot the ball. We were wrong because we were only thinking about these skills in their most traditional sense.

The contest was not about who had the best form or who could throw or shoot in a traditional game. The contest was to see how many of those footballs you could get through the little hole in 30 seconds or how many small basketballs you could get through the miniature basket in a minute. The game wasn't about accuracy. The game wasn't about form. The game was about volume. If we were going to win this game we had to think about it differently. We had to see the game with new eyes.

Part of the process of renewing the memberships in our individual lives or with the teams and organizations we serve is to create a new vision for our future. The process begins with reconnecting to the mission and purpose of our core priorities and then moves us into letting go of the baggage that weighs us down. The next step along the path is to imagine a new vision for our future—to recast new goals for the journey ahead. To grow beyond the way things were yesterday, we're going to have to see the road ahead with slightly new eyes. We're going to have to be willing to do something new. It might just be time to put on your new eyes.

You may need a bigger bike

This was a tremendous summer for riding bikes as a family. Our middle child, Benton, has progressed so much in his abilities over the last couple of months that his confidence has skyrocketed.

But lately, we've hit a new challenge: it's already time for a bigger bike. His little legs have grown so much in the last six months that he has outgrown the bike he worked so hard to master. Have you ever tried to ride a bike that's too small for you? You can't fully leverage your strength and ride the way you naturally should be able to. It is almost comical to watch his knees up high and cranking harder and harder to keep up with the other riders. So, it was time to go up a size!

This happens in our career lives as well. We work so hard to master a particular skill or way of doing things. We work hard to approach mastery and operate at the point where it becomes second nature. But, over time, even when we have become proficient, our skill doesn't fully serve us (or the team) anymore. The environment changes, the operation becomes stale, or a new skill is required. Eventually, we need a bigger bike. It's time to see things with new eyes and cast a new vision.

There is always a new challenge awaiting us–a new new opportunity for growth. Sometimes we get to choose the new bike to ride, sometimes it is given to us, and sometimes it is even broken. Other times it becomes obvious to everyone that you have outgrown the same old bike. It's time to change.

If you or someone on your team is feeling a little stuck, frustrated,

vision (noun): something you imagine, the ability to see ahead

or anxious about where you are on your current

path, perhaps it's time to adjust some things. Maybe it's time to re-vision for your next steps, open up to a new challenge, learn something, and find opportunities for growth. Consider this: you may just need a bigger bike!

Step back from the baggage claim

In 2008, I made the decision to quit my job. Many people around me wanted to know exactly what I was thinking. I wouldn't change my ten years as Director of Camp Akita and as the leader of mission projects locally and around the globe for anything. That work contained some of the most meaningful moments of my life and I will miss those days always. So it wasn't surprising, I guess, to have so many people come out of the woodwork and want to go have a cup of coffee, grab a beer, or sit together for lunch. Are you sure you're okay? Tell me what's really going on. You're saying you're quitting your job and you honestly don't know what you're going to do next?

Yep.

I loved those ten years of my life, but I also knew it was time for me to do something different, to try out my skills in new ways, to expand and to grow. I knew it would take courage to let go to be available for something new.

I knew that I needed to release my hold on a comfortable part of my life to make room for what was coming next. The one thing I did know is that I wanted to continue to do work with great purpose and to make sure that the spirit of my work was rooted in making a difference in the world. That mission was my compass. I knew there was something else coming but I wasn't exactly sure what it was. I needed space to recast, rethink, re-imagine what was possible next. It was going to take seeing things through new eyes.

I didn't know that it was going to lead me to the airport where I would end up spending seven days traveling to seven different cities studying people and then writing the book *Step Back from the Baggage Claim*. I didn't know so many wonderful things would emerge. I didn't know my observations and reflections would resonate so widely. I didn't know I would be asked to share this spirit in speeches for corporations, churches, nonprofits, small businesses, universities, and conferences around the world to explore the ideas of Stepping Back, the needs of 21st Century Leadership, Organizational Culture, Service and Creativity. And I didn't know that I would found Step Back Leadership Consulting LLC and now partner with individuals, teams, and organizations to add value and support their leadership development, culture, and mission and vision for their future. I wouldn't have known or experienced any of those things if I hadn't been rooted in purpose, willing to let go, cast a new vision—and leap. I'm glad I did. After 10 years of a wonderful role, a new path has emerged that challenges me to grow, learn, and lead in new and powerful ways.

Let's go shopping

Tesco, a British multinational grocery and general merchandise retailer, has been the third-largest retailer in the world measured by revenues (behind Walmart and Carrefour) and the second-largest measured in profits (behind Walmart). Beyond the UK, they are in 14 countries across Asia as well as Europe and North America. They are unique for many reasons, but most notably for their innovations.

Despite their strong footing in the market in many areas around the world in the mid-2000s, they began to notice a trend growing in areas of Asia, particularly in South Korea. The country is ranked as one of the hardest-working in the entire world, based on the number of hours South Koreans work in an average day. Based on the data, they are as busy and distracted as anyone else. The data showed that the number of hours average South Koreans worked per week combined with the longer time spent waiting for subway commutes left people with fewer pockets of time to do their grocery shopping. Fewer physical minutes in the grocery store does not lead to growth and is alarming for any retail business.

Tesco needed to change the way they looked at the situation. They needed to cast a new vision for their future. They had to innovate if they were going to reach the growing demands and reality of their culture. They needed to adapt.

The idea? Rather than wait for the average consumer to have enough time to enter their store, Tesco brought the grocery store to the people. Perhaps their most successful outcome was creating a virtual grocery store on the walls of the subway stations. The exact image of what it would look like when standing at a section of the physical store was replicated and placed on the subway walls. In the midst of their busy days as people waited for their trains to arrive, they could shop with their smartphones! Commuters could walk around "shopping" by scanning the QR codes of the items they wanted to purchase. Each item went into their virtual online basket until they were ready to "check out." Once they hit send, the order was placed and the groceries were set to be delivered right to their doors at the time they determined.

The results were staggering. The number of users shifting their habits to use this technology rose in the first month by 76 percent, and online sales increased by more than 130 percent! To truly meet the needs and desires of their customers, they shifted the way they looked at their business. They blazed a new trail.

Henry Ford, founder of the Ford Motor Company, was once asked in the early days of the automobile's existence about how he knew what people wanted or needed in the future. His response, "If I would have asked people what they wanted, they would have said that they wanted a bigger horse." Sometimes we need to cast a vision that takes us beyond what we currently can see.

A running conversation my wife Amy and I have is centered on the question, "What is the life we are trying to create?" Not only is it a powerful question for us, but it is also a question we return to often. We try to gain clarity on the vision we have for our lives. We try to be thoughtful and purposeful about who we want to be and what we're about. We need to make time to see where our separate visions can be blended together. We want to return to the question in order to cast a new vision for our future (because visions and futures do change). What we envisioned at age 25 differed from what our vision was at 35, and so on.

Even though it is years away, I have become enamored lately with the retirement ages of life. Not because I yearn to be there, but I think of it as an interesting time of life. Watching my parents and many other couples in their sixties, seventies, and eighties move into this phase of life is fascinating to me. It is interesting to watch them navigate their way into this new time of their lives and break through the images of what they always thought it would feel like to retire. I love sitting and hearing them respond to the question, "What is the life you are trying to create now?" Undoubtedly, it feels a little different than they imagined, there are challenges they might not have expected, but there is also tremendous opportunity to experience something from a new perspective. The process of recasting the vision for our lives never ends until we're unwilling to cast it any differently or live into it. It is exceedingly liberating to me to realize that we all have the power to recast our vision for our lives and step into new chapters of health, happiness, focus, and learning. We all have the ability to write a new script for how we choose to live today and tomorrow. We all have a choice in the life we live.

Our F'ing problem

So why do we stay stuck repeating the same patterns for so long and keep our hand caught in the monkey trap?

Well, we have an F'ing problem. We F<u>orget</u>. We forget the purposeful life that we want to live. We forget the life that is awaiting us. We forget we have the ability to cast a new vision. We forget we have the ability to respond to new chapters with new resolve.

A friend of mine, John Rue, reminds me of our F'ing problem all the time. He is one of the consultants with Built to Lead, a firm with a passion for transforming leaders and organizations. We often have conversations about how easy it is for individuals and organizations to get stuck in the rat race, "forgetting" their deeper purpose and passions. Because we have never lived in a more distracted, complex, and busy time than now, we are tricked into just doing the same thing again and again. As Albert Einstein reminded us, "The definition of insanity is doing the same thing over and over again and expecting a different result."

The fact is that doing the same thing over and over again is often the easiest thing to do. We have our routines. We know what to expect. We know how things are going to play out. Life stays "normal." Familiar. The easiest thing for Tesco to have done was to stay right where they were. After all, they were still the third-largest grocery chain in the world.

In Tesco's most honest moments and in our most honest moments, we know we desire more. In the memberships in our life, we know that going on "as is" doesn't always lead to continued commitment and enthusiasm. That's why the process of renewing our memberships is so critical. It reminds us of the beauty we have right here and now, and the feeling of empowerment gained by actively participating in a growing and new reality. Even in moments when we are standing still, if we're rooted in purpose and open to our authentic self, we are growing in ways that can't help but move us forward. We all have the ability to adapt like Tesco.

While writing this book, I have gone through a few months of neck and shoulder pain. Long hours on the computer in the same position and in different hotel beds when I'm on the road speaking and consulting are part of what caused this situation. My neck has become so stiff at times that I have needed a massage therapist to help work the knotted muscles out. Recently after one of the sessions, the therapist said to me, "You need to find ways to break your habits and periodically take time to stretch your neck and shoulders. Your muscles are getting used to these painful positions. They are becoming what they know."

Talk about a powerful image! The habits we form and the modes of operation we are used to can become the new normals we experience. If we want to change, if we want to grow, if we want to create something new, we're going to have to break those habits and stretch.

It is possible

As I alluded to earlier, basketball was very important to me growing up. I loved the game from a very early age and worked extremely hard to be the best I could be. As a skinny little kid, I was always dreaming about the games I couldn't wait to play in and the magical moments that players want to be a part of. I can't tell you how many shots I took with the clock winding down in my head as I envisioned hitting the game-winning shot. Some of my fondest memories in my life have happened in a gym, on a playground, or as a part of a team. I have been blessed to experience some amazing moments and achievements from grade school through college. The game has given me and taught me more than I can express.

In sports, your senior year in high school is a very special time because of the relationship with your teammates and your final go-around, this time as the veterans. I had a vision of our team being great, not just good. I remember many magical moments from that final season. We upset the consensus Number 1 team in the city, Eastmoor Academy, much to the surprise of many. We beat the consensus Number 1 team in our league, Westerville North, on their home floor. Despite a couple of losses, we ended the season just behind Westerville North in our league and were ranked Number 5 in Columbus, Ohio. By all normal standards, it was a very successful season, and individually, as one of the co-captains of the team and all-league performer, I had a lot to celebrate.

But, oh, do the losses hurt. Despite the many accolades and celebrations, there is always a next game. We were upset in the first round of the district tournament by a team we were beating by eight points with only a minute to play. Some great plays by the other team and poor decisions down the stretch by our team cost us the chance for the magical tournament run I had envisioned. I missed a couple of shots at the end that could have won it for our team. It was devastating. I had spent so much time thinking about hitting those shots, had made them in other games, but this time they didn't go in. It's amazing how often I still think about that game. Even with the terrific regular season that we had as a team and the wonderful personal accolades and awards I received as an individual, there still is that feeling of "what if?"

There were things I wanted to say to our team before the game that I didn't say. There was a mindset that we needed to go into that tournament that we didn't have. We didn't take the time to truly realize what was possible and recognize that it could all be over in an instant. And it was.

Our mindset going in was part of our downfall. Everyone (including me) had booked Spring Break trips well in advance of the tournament. A Spring Break trip presupposed that we would make it only a couple of rounds into the tournament. We talked ourselves into thinking it was okay by saying we could always change our plans if we get hot in the tournament, but subconsciously, we were thinking more about being on the beach with our friends.

I'll never forget sitting on the airplane on our way home from a fantastic Spring Break and looking at one of my best friends and co-captain from the team, David Kanuth. David had just spoken to his mom on the phone before boarding the plane to let her know we were all safe and had a great time. With disbelief on his face and what felt like slow motion, he turned to me and said, "Westerville North won the state championship."

I went numb. It was one of the strangest sensations I've felt in my life. It was like getting punched right in the face by the reality you missed a once-in-a-lifetime opportunity. It was over. I would have traded our great Spring Break trip in the blink of an eye for that opportunity again.

I guess I just assumed the winner of the state championship would be some distant team with powers beyond imagination. But not Westerville North. We had beaten Westerville North! We knew many of their players well. They were a very talented team, and I was thrilled for them. I called one of them in particular to congratulate him. But it was a tough reality for someone like me to swallow because in that moment it became clear: we never truly believed it was possible. We never took the time to take all of those dreams we all had growing up to honestly look at each other and say, "Let's go for it. Let's bring those dreams to life."

We never truly believed the vision was possible and that hurt as deeply as anything for me. I wish someone had grabbed us all before the tournament and slapped us around to help us realize that winning was possible. I wish that had been the most important thing on our minds. But, the reality is, we should have been slapping ourselves around. We should have owned our own lives and our own opportunities. It wasn't someone else's opportunity. It was ours. We got caught up in the moment and distracted by all the other things in our lives: accolades, girls, vacations, fun. We lost our focus and didn't even realize that this was our one shot.

I carry that memory with me as a reminder. It is a reminder to me—one I had to learn the hard way—that if we don't believe something is possible, then it probably isn't. It's a reminder that if there is something important to me or that I want to happen in my life, I have to be the first person to believe. I have to participate in the creation of that vision.

The memberships in my life deserve my belief. The belief in my marriage and the commitment to renew that membership in year 12 just as I did in year 11 (or remembering the covenant we committed to in year one). The belief in my relationship with my kids and the next steps in our journey together. The belief in my work, the messages I share about the lessons I've learned and the companies I am privileged to serve. The belief in the mission and vision of the organizations I serve, work for, or volunteer for. And if I don't believe in a membership anymore or I am not willing to commit or engage in the next leg of the journey or realize that something has just come to the end of its time and needs to change, I need to be honest and take personal responsibility for the changes needed.

But for those I do believe in and am willing to see with fresh eyes, whatever the vision is for how it can be developed, I must remember—It is Possible! Possibility starts with belief and leads to action.

"IT IS POSSIBLE."

Questions For Renewal

- *What in your life and work needs a new perspective or to be examined with new eyes?*

- *What is a Vision of the life you'd like to create in the next 12 months? What are you experiencing, doing, aiming for in your life and work? How do you see your "why" being actualized?*

- *Are there ways you could adapt and try something new that might be outside of conventional wisdom?*

- *When will you have an extended conversation with the key people in your life about the Vision, life, work or impact you're trying to create?*

Bias Toward Action (Not Busyness)

Three minutes of reflection:

- What is your vision or goal for today? This week? This month? This quarter? This year? As you gain clarity, remember — It Is Possible! What are one to three actions you can contribute today to begin to bring your Vision to life?

NOTES:

"The best time to plant a tree is 40 years ago.
The second best time is now." —Chinese Proverb

Chapter 5

BECOME A FIRST RESPONDER

The call came in the middle of the night. The kind of phone call that everyone dreads because you know the middle-of-the-night call is never good news. Howard Schultz, CEO of Starbucks Coffee, rolled over and answered the phone.

What he heard was that a gunman had broken into one of their Washington, D.C., stores and shot and killed three of the workers while attempting to rob the register. One of Starbucks' highest priorities is safety, and anyone who knows how they extend benefits even to their hourly employees realizes that Starbucks takes very seriously how they care for their people. Howard had to respond.

Within hours of the shooting, Howard Schultz was sitting with the families of the lost, with his other employees, with the community. He was there to tell them personally and directly how sorry he was that Starbucks was unable to keep them safe. He was there to respond. He was there to care. He was there because it was the right thing to do.

One of the great blessings of the last few years has been my relationship with Howard Behar, the former president of Starbucks. He is the one who first shared that story with me and gave me insight into the caring nature of some of their key leaders. He and I collaborated on the Business Leader Edition of *Step Back from the Baggage Claim*. He's been a tremendous support and mentor for me along the way and I look forward to our conference calls. It's always great to be with Howard.

I'll never forget one of the first things Howard shared with me about success in today's culture. We talked about success—not purely monetary success—but fulfilling a mission and vision you set out to achieve.

"Your success will not be defined by intricate business strategy," he began. "Business strategy and fundamentals are certainly critical, but your success will be defined by the way you respond to the obstacles, delays, and cancellations that show up along your path."

At first I thought he was talking only about my career pursuits or his experience leading Starbucks from 28 stores to 12,000 stores internationally, but finally I realized he was talking about any venture that is successful in today's culture. He was talking about the world we live in today and the necessity to respond when things don't go the way we had planned. The agility and response-ability to spring into action to meet needs and make progress. He was adamant that this is how they built Starbucks and this is how any successful entity has to be wired in the world today. The bottom line is that how we respond is everything.

Columbine

My uncle, Rick Barger, was the senior pastor at a church in Littleton, Colorado for 15 years. His work, approach, and spirit have had a tremendous influence on many people (including me).

Listening to him talk about the day the phone call came into his office from Columbine High School stops people in their tracks. As he was getting ready to head out for a lunch appointment, a call came into his office alerting him to what was happening at the school. In the midst of gun fire and panic, calls for help to anyone who would listen were being made. He immediately rushed to the school.

He was one of the first civilians to witness the scene at the high school when the first batch of students came rushing out of the building in disarray, disbelief, and hysteria. He immediately began hugging students, getting them to a safe spot, and handing them his cell phone to call their parents and let them know they were safe. To listen to him describe the way the community was flipped upside down that day is heart-wrenching. During the rest of that day students were ushered to other school buildings where parents awaited to see if their child would arrive.

His church was packed that night with the only possible response: to create a place where kids, parents, the community could hold each other in their arms and just be together. The first step toward healing was to respond. At the darkest time in that community's existence, they knew they had to respond with the light and spirit of a loving, but sorrowful, God.

It became very clear in the days, weeks, and months following Columbine that the response was not a one-time thing. Responding was a process. Responding was about showing up each day. These kids, this school, this community, and this country had much more to process and respond to. We still do.

Whether it's a tragedy like Columbine, a devastating earthquake or other natural disaster, a divorce, a firing at work, a diagnosis of a disease or illness—or even the loss of a game, project, job, boyfriend or girlfriend, we know that the immediate response is critical but isn't sufficient by itself. It takes a commitment over the long haul to loving, caring, serving, persevering, and adapting to the challenges that show up along the way. Responding is leadership in action.

First responders

The term "First Responders" has unfortunately become all too common in our daily lexicon in the last few years. Terrorist attacks, domestic violence, school shootings, and natural disasters around the world have put that term into our lives. In the midst of unbelievable tragedy, trauma, and evil, we have witnessed the heroic efforts of so many ordinary people who responded in the blink of an eye. Their courage and servant leadership at some of the darkest moments have reminded us of the power of good in the world. Their light has kept the darkness from overwhelming us all.

I've often imagined how I would respond if thrust into one of those awful situations, but it also caused me to think about what it means to be a First Responder. It's made me think about other situations in my life that are far less dramatic. It has caused me to pause and think about the courageous conversations that are needed with people in my life. It has caused me to think about what it means to be a First Responder with my children and what I want that response to be. It caused me to think about being a First Responder for my wife and challenged me to think more deeply about the responses needed before issues even surface. It has enlightened me to how critical it is within our faith community to have First Responders who are able to help the congregation remember and refocus on the heart of the ministry. It has inspired me to think about what it means for leaders to be First Responders in their organizations to show others the very best of what it means to be a leader. I have witnessed how powerful it is within a business culture when it becomes part of the DNA of the team members to be First Responders. Our communities, our organizations, and every single team in the world is in need of First Responders. Are you a First Responder?

Point A to Point Z

As Stephen Covey reminded us, our "Response-Ability" is critical. We all have the ability to respond, and it isn't about a one-time thing. Within our memberships, the only way visions are changed or realized is by the small, thoughtful actions of many. For many of the clients I work with, I'm not only helping to support the development and culture of their leadership teams, but I am also helping them gain clarity about their vision for the future and the action steps needed to stimulate progress. It is fantastic to help a leadership team blend their strengths, renew their vision, and develop a communication plan to engage their people. This is some of the most important work any successful entity does.

I remind them of the Japanese proverb, "Vision without action is a daydream. Action without vision is a nightmare." Progress takes both, and most of us need a process to help us take the time to explore, develop, plan, and lead anything of significance.

One of the most common missteps in any kind of visioning exercise is that we jump so quickly to casting that new vision for the future and dreaming and articulating the end point, Point Z of our plan, that we forget to identify where we actually are at the starting point, Point A. In fact, it isn't uncommon for a team to have several people disagree with where Point A even is. Therefore, it's critical that we first step back and assess where Point A is—where we are currently—before we launch into the exercises and processes necessary to define Point Z. That's why I began this book by discussing the need to weed through the distractions and remember where we are before casting a new vision for what could be.

The other misstep in any visioning process once we establish a good understanding of where Point A is and feel conviction and clarity on where we want to be at Point Z, is to leap from A to Z in one huge jump. It is also very common for team members to get overwhelmed by thinking about all of the work, planning, and implementation it will take to get from Point A to Point Z. All of a sudden, this exciting new vision has become an extremely daunting and anxiety-filled pursuit. As a result, it's easier to go back to what we know and what we did yesterday. That's why the vision, clarity of next actions, and commitment to the journey are so important.

These challenges are very common for all kinds of groups and relationships. Designing a vision that blends different perspectives is tough but powerful work. It involves all that we're talking about in this book (without these things it's easy to get stuck).

When I'm working with an organization, I often explain that I'm not sure I believe in "long-range planning" anymore. You know, the monumental and laborious task that so many groups go through to create the binder that outlines every single action they are going to take in the next seven to ten years. What usually happens to that binder filled with all of that time, resources, and energy? That's right, it goes up on a shelf until it is time to do it all again years down the road.

What I do believe in are "long-range visions" and short-term plans." We do need to take the time, contribute the resources, and commit to the discovery of the vision and buy-in that the dreams are possible. We do need to be able to paint a picture of what we want that new reality to look like, what will be different, and most importantly, why we want to go there. All of these elements are critical to the vision. But, we don't have to have every single item figured out for how we're going to operate and what is going to happen in Year Eight—*because we don't know*. And it's okay to admit it.

We need a vision of the future that compels us toward action. Then we need to get really good at executing the short-term plans that move us closer to that vision. The way we deal with an overwhelming or daunting experience with the vision is to chop it up in bite-sized pieces. We don't need to go from Point A to Z all in one move. We only need to go first from Point A to Point B. I help groups boil the task down and think about it in terms of their three-month plan, their six-month plan, and their 12-month plan. Each individual, team, and organization has its own unique culture and structure, so we work together to establish what will be most effective to implement first. There is no cookie-cutter solution. Just a commitment to the process and response that compels action.

It's now time for my final basketball analogy. Mike Krzyzewski Head Men's Basketball Coach at Duke University, already is recognized as one of the greatest coaches in the history of the game. Year in and year out his system has produced winning results. His leadership style and philosophies also have been widely discussed and appreciated by leaders of all industries and organizations.

Just recently on the radio I heard an interview with Coach K. He was questioned by the host, "How do you keep building a winning team every year?"

"It's not about building a winning team. It's about building a winning culture," Coach K

> **culture** (noun): the way you think, act, and interact as part of a group

responded. "We don't focus on building a winning team; we're focused on the culture. Building a winning culture takes day-in and day-out focus on who we want to be, focus on where we're trying to go, and the discipline to work and take the next step, together. If you build a winning culture, a winning team will follow."

I say to groups I work with that one of the greatest efforts they can make today is to define and clarify the culture they want to be a part of. The efforts to define *how* they expect to lead every day, compete every day, and live every day are more responsible for their success than anything else. There is no better use of our time as a family, a team, an organization, or a couple than to define and clarify *why* we're doing this, *where* we're trying to go, *how* we're committed to work to get there, and *what* we're going to do next in response of those goals. Our commitment to that winning culture breeds a winning experience.

Coach K also made this important point with conviction: "Losing is easy. It only takes one person on a team that doesn't buy-in to the vision, isn't willing to work, or doesn't contribute to the culture."

We never truly know how we will react in moments when tragedy or crisis strikes. But, we all do have the opportunity to prepare for how we *hope* to respond in the days ahead in our lives. We won't always be perfect and certainly will stumble along the way, but the clarity of how we hope to respond does serve us. It helps to paint the vision for the culture we are trying to create. It gives us something to aim for. It gives us somewhere to focus our eyes.

Right now the memberships in our life and work are waiting for our responses. No actions are silver-bullet solutions that solve everything, but there are responses that matter. There are conversations waiting to be had and gestures that are needed. Every time we put caring, compassionate, clear actions into motion for someone around us, it makes a difference. That's how the culture is built—one thoughtful and intentional act at a time.

And the winning usually follows.

"Vision without action is a daydream.

Action without vision is a nightmare."

- Japanese Proverb

Questions For Renewal

- *Who needs your response right now in your life and work?*
- *When has someone in your life responded for you with spirit, care and leadership that made an impact on you?*
- *In what ways can you put service, care and leadership into action for the people and strangers in your life and work?*
- *What are the next actions needed to respond to the changes that are happening around you?*
- *How will you respond today?*

Bias Toward Action (Not Busyness)

Three minutes of reflection:

- Write a note, make a call, or swing by to share a message with someone who may need your "response" right now in their life.
- Make a list that consists of one response that is needed in each significant area of your life —your work, your family, your friendships, your faith, your community.

NOTES:

ReMember

To Own It

"We can throw stones, complain about them,
stumble on them, climb over them,
or choose to build with them."
—William Arthur Ward

Chapter 6

DARE TO BEGIN

I have an image of the stuntman Evel Knievel etched in my brain. I can still see the long row of buses lined up that he was attempting to jump, the ramp lit with flames from torches, and the red, white, and blue cape draped over his shoulders, as the infamous stuntman revved his motorcycle engine. Billowing clouds of smoke lifted into the air as his motorcycle raced down the long runway, up the ramp, and then flew through the air for what was an unimaginable amount of time.

To a child born in the mid-Seventies, Evel Knievel was an icon. He was the first true daredevil and stunt performer to capture the attention and imagination of the America of my youth. In his career he attempted more than 75 ramp-to-ramp jumps on motorcycles and entered *The Guinness Book of World Records* for "most bones broken in a lifetime" with a total of 433. He had many unsuccessful high-profile jumps that led to severe injuries and near death. To some, he was a real-life superhero. To most, he was an absolute nutcase.

I believe our world today is in need of daredevils. In some ways I think the term leadership has been muddied in the clutter of the world lately too. As a culture, we were tricked into believing that leadership was about having the fancy title, being the person on the top, and getting to tell everyone else what to do. Fortunately, we are evolving to realize that the most compelling leaders in the world today are those who bring specific attributes, mindsets, and actions to life. The best leaders follow their core values and live them out with action. One of the most requested topics I speak to groups about is a model for leadership in the 21st century and seven key attributes for leaders of today. It's fun to flip the traditional model of leadership on its head and dive into what it means to be a Servant Leader, Storyteller, Collaborator, Innovator, Daredevil, Adaptor, Global Citizen. Each of these attributes is present in the best leaders throughout the world and is critical to building compelling teams, cultures, and impacting the world.

For this spot in the book, however, it's appropriate to highlight one attribute in particular. I believe the very best leaders today are the ones who have a bit of daredevil in them. Not a reckless daredevil (as many would suggest Knievel was) who puts himself or others around him in danger, but a daredevil who lives with a deeply courageous spirit —one not afraid to challenge the status quo. When I think about the challenges we face in the 21st century, the pace at which things are moving, and the opportunities to infuse positive change to the world around us, I know it's going to take some daring, courageous leadership from all of us.

Our fears, doubts, and security have a funny way of imprisoning us. They can surround us and keep us from doing anything that would rock the boat. Anything that might move us out of our comfort zone gets put on the back burner. We'll deal with it later, we say.

But the words of the poet, Eugene Ware, ring in my ears: "All glory comes from daring to begin."

When I think about the relationships, commitments, work, and memberships in my life, I can't help thinking about how I want to dare to lead next. I think about my work, and I know there is authentic work that needs the courageous nudge forward. I think about the people I partner and collaborate with, and I know we will need courage to go where we haven't gone before. I think about my marriage, and I know there are courageous conversations and efforts that will allow Amy and me to grow and mature into the future. I think about my parents getting older, and I know courage will be required for some of the moments and choices that will inevitably arrive. I think about my children, and I know that I'm going to have to dare to let our relationships evolve as they move through the stages of life. I think about my faith, and I know that I want to be open to new ways that God is working within my life. I want to engage in my memberships. I want to lead and to serve.

I have to be willing to dare to begin.

Put your name on the door

She was giddy as a school girl. She bubbled with excitement as she bounced back and forth on her toes, a dance ready to break out at any point. A smile stretched ear to ear and her eyes glowed. It wasn't the typical scene you see from most employees in the hall of a large company.

The big news was that she had just been told she was was moving from a cubicle desk to a real-life office with her name on the door. A fairly small event in the big picture of the world, but hugely significant in meaning to this young woman. The move communicated validation, appreciation, and a kind of permanence she hadn't experienced in her five years of working for the company. With her name on the door, this space was now hers to own. She belonged and mattered in a way she felt she hadn't before.

The differences between renting and owning are pretty significant, not just in the economic sense, but also in our mindset. One is temporary, and one takes the longer view. This young woman wasn't renting the space, but had had an underlying feeling she was just borrowing it for a while. The affirmation this dedicated space brought her was real. It energized her in ways she hadn't imagined.

A couple of years ago I had the distinct pleasure of visiting the headquarters of Southwest

Airlines in Dallas, Texas. I was given a tour and the opportunity to learn a little bit about the company's culture and the way they develop their people. It was a fun and impressive day spent with their staff.

Lining the hallways of their entire facility are memorabilia that commemorate their history. From the cocktail-napkin drawing where the plan for Southwest Airlines was conceived to life-size models of the different uniforms the flight attendants have worn over the years to every newspaper clipping or magazine headline about the company, Southwest's heritage and success are celebrated. There was a very upbeat, positive, and fun atmosphere with everyone you crossed paths with in the building. That day, it also wasn't uncommon to see one of the employees riding down the hallway on a scooter.

Perhaps the thing that stuck out to me the most though was one statement that appeared everywhere. I mean *everywhere*. It was on posters covering the walls. It was on buttons people were wearing. It was on a plaque in the center of tables. I would have bet that some of the employees had it tattooed on their foreheads! The message was loud and clear. It read in big words,

"Count on me to OWN IT. We are all ambassadors of our culture."

We were told that these words are shared with every new employee from Day One. The message implies that there are many, many, many people who apply for a job at Southwest Airlines, but if you want to work here, the company has to be able to count on you to *own it*. They show prospective employees the list of Southwest's very specific core values and the vision for the company. Those who want to work there have to *own* this vision and be willing to respond every day with actions that bring it to life. All are ambassadors of their culture.

We all have to be willing to own our roles in the memberships in our lives. We have to find time and space to filter out the distractions, take stock of the memberships in our life, remember the mission and purpose of each, release the baggage that is weighing us down, cast a new vision for how we're going to contribute to strengthen our memberships in the future, and then respond by putting compelling action into motion. Again, I'm saying this as much to myself as I am to you. We have to own the growth of these memberships and do so by going through the renewal process of remembering. One step at a time. Point A to B to C to D. We have to be the best ambassador of the culture we're looking for on our teams, in our companies, in our marriages, in our families, with our friends, and in the communities we serve. If we don't *own it*, then it probably isn't possible.

Jack Welch, former Chairman and CEO of General Electric, once said, "Success is less a function of grandiose predictions than it is a result of being able to respond rapidly to the changes as they occur."

As the changes occur (and they inevitably will) throughout all of the different memberships in our lives, our success will come from our initial response of care, love, and action and then be sustained by our commitment to the process of responding over the long haul. How will you begin to respond? Will you *own* it?

Bathe every day

Zig Ziglar, whom I mentioned earlier, had just finished a speech. Fired up with excitement and inspiration from Ziglar's talk, a man in the audience stood up to ask a question. He cited ways in which he knew he would take messages of the speech and implement them into his life and business. But the questioner admitted he wasn't sure about this whole "motivation" thing and went on to explain to Ziglar that his motivational feeling from the events always seemed to fade away.

"People often say that motivation doesn't last," Ziglar said in his response. Of course it doesn't last, he continued, but "neither does bathing. That's why we recommend it daily."

We bathe daily because we get dirty daily. We eat daily because

> **ambassador** (noun): an authorized representative, messenger

our bodies need food daily. Motivation is no different. Ziglar explained that even he—someone who gave motivational speeches for a living—needed to find new ways to stay motivated.

We can't simply take a shot in the arm or a few pills of motivation that last us forever. We have to find new ways to motivate ourselves each day, to remember the purpose we're trying to accomplish, the new vision we are casting, and the ways we hope to respond with action in the world. We have to roll up our sleeves every day and be courageous enough to take the next step. Slowly, progress is made and amazing things are accomplished. But it begins with opening our eyes every day and seeing the opportunities to lead.

Remembering tiptoes

It's one of my favorite moments in life right now. The sound of tiptoes comes pitter-pattering down the hallway, and I can hear her blanket being dragged along the carpet with each little step. My eyes are closed as I lie peacefully in bed, but I hear every stealthy move she makes. Our youngest child, Brooke (four years old), has decided it's time to start the day. You wouldn't think this would be such a celebrated daily moment for parents of three young kids. After all, sleep is powerful currency.

However, there is something magical about those few minutes that begin each day. Brooke's hair is matted to her head, pillow imprints sprawl clear across her tiny face, and her overall appearance is of a disheveled little person. A cute one at that. She grabs daddy's hand and we walk down to our family room to begin the ritual.

She crawls right up on my lap and drapes her arms around me as if it's been forever since we've last been together. She needs Daddy (but I think Daddy really needs her more). It's a common scene, but this morning the dialogue was priceless.

"Brookie, do you know that Daddy loves you?" I whispered, breaking the rhythm of her deep breaths against my neck.

She leaned back and a giant smile overtook her sleepy face. Her beautiful blue eyes and straggly blonde hair radiated with her giggly response, "Why do you have to always tell me that, Daddy?" she exclaimed with the accent on the word 'always'.

"Because I just want to remind you, Brookie."

"Daddy, I won't ever forget that. Ever."

It was a heart-stealing moment I wish I could bottle forever. It came from a four-year-old, but it was layered with such wisdom and beauty. It was cute, innocent, sacred, and ... somewhat true. Somewhat true?

I have great faith that she will always know I love her. I have tremendous hope that I will be a part of a million more moments throughout her life that cement my love even more deeply within her. But, I also know the reality of the busy world we live in today. With each passing day, her life will become more full with activities, pursuits, relationships, accomplishments, failures, obligations, responsibilities, commitments, and distractions. Each day will bring new challenges and plenty of events that can keep us from experiencing those sacred moments. It will become even more important for her to be reminded—for both of us to acknowledge and remember our foundational love. We will have to remember to practice putting our focus on the *why* of our relationship.

Whether it's our relationships with our children, spouses, friends, co-workers, clients, faith, or the causes and organizations we support, our success and fulfillment are directly defined by our ability to bring our best selves to the moment at hand. I believe it takes an intentional and proactive mindset.

Survino

His name was Survino (pronounced sir-vee-no). He was a bellhop at the hotel where I stayed in Kuala Lumpur last year. I was in Malaysia for a couple of speeches, and Survino was the one constant of every day I was there.

As soon as the elevator would open and I would make my way into the hotel lobby, Survino came trotting from clear across the other side of the room. It was a large hotel with very high ceilings and an expansive lobby. Without fail, Survino would make his way directly through the masses and right up to me.

"Mr. Jason, Mr. Jason, how are you today?" he would always begin with such a gentle but upbeat tone.

"I'm doing just fine, Survino. How are you today?" I would respond.

"Oh, I am well, Mr. Jason. Is there anything I can do for you today to make your stay better?"

Most days I would just laugh and let Survino know I was fine and didn't need anything. But still, each time he saw me, the experience would be repeated. One day I did need to track down some sunscreen (because I was a pale white guy in Malaysia) and Survino began to literally walk me down the street to show me where to go. I thanked him and assured him I could find my way.

The reason I mention Survino is because he was one of 40 bellhops—one of 40 other people in a role similar to his, yet I can't tell you anything about the rest of them. I certainly can't tell you their names, and I definitely don't have their email address (as I have Survino's).

Survino was special because he remembered a couple of pretty simple things that he brought to life every day: 1) He remembered the purpose of his hotel was to provide an exceptional customer experience for those who stayed there. 2) He remembered how simple but powerful it is to take the time to learn someone's name and make them feel welcomed. 3) He remembered how important it is to go out of your way to serve the mission.

Most important, he "ReMembered" each day. He renewed his commitment to his role and responded with simple but compelling action. Of all the employees in the entire hotel, Survino took ownership of the culture. He was the greatest ambassador they could imagine.

One person with passion

The English novelist E.M. Forster said, "One person with passion is better than forty people merely interested."

That quote has been haunting me in all the good ways this year (and certainly reminding me of Survino). Am I going to be passionate about my wife and my role in our marriage? Am I going to be a passionate father? Am I going to be a person of passion with the clients and organizations I'm lucky to serve? Am I going to engage in the organizations and causes I belong to? Am I passionate about the memberships in my life or am I merely interested?

We all make daily choices about how we engage with the memberships in our lives. We know that the easiest thing to do is maintain the status quo. The easiest thing to do is take the path of least resistance. But when we are rooted in love, care, progress, growth, and authentic leadership in the world, the path of merely being interested is never enough. I choose passion.

This book is an invitation to us all to embrace and engage the memberships in our lives with passion. It's an invitation to look at the team we are working with right now at our job and consider what actions are needed to renew and recommit our focus. It is an invitation for all of us to think about the relationships in our lives and choose how we need to respond to those around us. It is an invitation for us to pause in the midst of a distracting world and remember where we want to put our eyes, give our hearts, and lead.

We have the ability to infuse a human element filled with gratitude, compassion, leadership, and service into every one of our memberships. Not perfectly, I know, but we have the capability to provide the voice and to lead with action. We have the privilege to share the human element with others.

So, what is the appropriate way to end this book? Well, probably with a reminder. As you wake up each day, I invite you to practice remembering these five things:

1) **RePurpose:** — Return to the Mission

2) **ReLease:** — Let go of your baggage

3) **ReCast:** — Create a new vision for the future

4) **ReSpond:** — Put compelling action into motion

5) **Own It:** — Dare to live the life you want

When we remember these messages every day in a distracting world, we ReMember: we actively recommit to our most precious memberships, relationships, and work in the world.

Perhaps it's time to renew our memberships. Dare to begin.

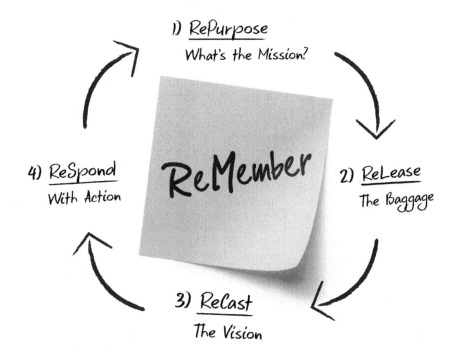

Where You Look Is Where You Go!

10 Conversation Starters
For Different Memberships In Your Life

Your Team or Business

- *What is our Mission? What's compelling about our purpose?*
- *Are we busy or effective? Where are we being most effective in actualizing our purpose?*
- *What is stealing our attention individually, as a team, or as an entire organization?*
- *Do we take Purposeful Breaks to reconnect our people to the mission and vision?*
- *What's the baggage (Events, Consequences, Thoughts) that is weighing us down? What baggage do we need to let go of and what do we need to address?*
- *Is there a "this is how we've always done it" that needs to be released?*
- *What is the new vision for what we're trying to create in the next 12 months? What are the top three priorities we must act on next?*
- *How do we define our culture? What are the core values we want to bring to life?*
- *What leadership attributes does our team need to be successful? How are we developing and strengthening those attributes?*
- *How could we own the vision for this team? What does it look like to be a person of passion? Are we willing to renew this membership?*

Your Significant Relationships / Marriage

- *What's the purpose of this relationship? Why did we choose to be in relationship with each other?*
- *What have we agreed to in this covenant? Where are we being effective in bringing that covenant to life? Where are we falling short of our agreement?*
- *What is distracting us from investing our best into this relationship?*
- *What is the baggage (Events, Consequences, Thoughts) we are carrying in this relationship right now? What do we need to release and what needs to be dealt with in a healthier way?*
- *What is the vision we have for our relationship and the life we want to create moving forward? How would we articulate the kind of relationship we want to have?*
- *What actions, pursuits, interests or experiences bring out the best in our relationship?*
- *How do we want to spend our time, money, talents, spirit?*
- *What are three requests we have for our partner that would bring joy, honor, and healthy connection to the relationship? Are we both willing to honor the requests we have?*
- *What might we dare to begin next together? How could we break our routines to infuse creativity and new experiences into our journey?*
- *How can we take greater ownership on the road ahead? Are we willing to renew this membership?*

156

Your Membership Organization

- *Why does this organization exist? What's the purpose and mission?*
- *Why was I/we compelled to join this organization?*
- *What is keeping me/us from increasing the level of engagement?*
- *What is the baggage (Events, Consequences, Thoughts) I/we are carrying that is getting in the way of fulfilling our mission or experience? What needs to be released or addressed so that I/we are able to move into the future?*
- *What commitments or projects have served their purpose, are not functioning effectively, or don't have the support they need to go on?*
- *What is possible for the future of this organization? What opportunities exist to strengthen the effectiveness of the mission and excitement for the future?*
- *How do you see yourself contributing to the organization next? What time, talents, finances, spirit, and energy do you have to contribute?*
- *What does it mean to be a First Responder for this organization or community? Am I/we responding with the heart of a servant leader?*
- *How would we describe the culture of our organization? What core values or attributes of leadership would we like to strengthen within our group?*
- *What will we dare to begin next? Am I committed to renewing this membership?*

* Email Info@BookRemember.com to request a free one page PDF discussion guide for your book club or team meeting. Request a discussion guide specific for : Business Teams, Nonprofit Organizations, Bible Studies, or Marriages.

Resources

- Barger, Jason, Step Back from the Baggage Claim, One Love Publishers, 2008, 2010, 2011, 2012.
- Lubbock, Sir John, http://www.brainyquote.com/quotes/quotes/j/johnlubboc107112.html
- The Multitasking Paradox, Harvard Business Review, March 2013, P.30-31.
- Slow Down to Speed Up, Forbes, John B. McGuire and Vance Tang, http://www.forbes.com/2011/02/23/slow-down-speed-efficiency-leadership-managing-ccl.html
- Kennedy, John F., http://www.brainyquote.com/quotes/quotes/j/johnfkenn164001.html
- Ziglar, Zig, http://www.movemequotes.com/legends/zig-ziglar/.
- Collins, James and Porras, Jerry. Built to Last. New York, New York. HarperCollins Publishers, 1994, 1997, 2002.
- Tzu, Lao, https://www.goodreads.com/quotes/10651-when-i-let-go-of-what-i-am-i-become
- The Biggest Loser, http://www.biggestloser.com.
- Walsh, Neale Donald, http://blog.gaiam.com/quotes/authors/neale-donald-walsch
- How I Did It.., Harvard Business Review, January-February 2013, P.39-42.
- Campbell, Joseph, http://www.oprah.com/quote/Quote-About-Letting-Go-Joseph-Campbell-Quote
- Rogers, Aaron, http://en.wikipedia.org/wiki/Aaron_Rodgers
- Finding Joe, Patrick Solomon, 2011, www.findingjoethemovie.com
- Dyer, Wayne, http://quotables.quora.com/When-we-change-the-way-we-look-at-things-the-things-we-look-at-change-Wayne-Dyer

- Tesco (LSE: TSCO), http://www.tesco.com, http://www.youtube.com/watch?v=fGaVFRzTTP4
- Einstein, Albert, http://www.brainyquote.com/quotes/quotes/a/alberteins133991.html
- Chinese Proverb, http://thinkexist.com/quotation/the_best_time_to_plant_a_tree_is_twenty_years_ago/254949.html
- Behar, Howard. It's Not About the Coffee. New York, New York. The Penguin Group, 2007, 2009.
- Covey, Stephen, https://www.stephencovey.com/7habits/7habits-habit1.php
- Japanese Proverb, http://thinkexist.com/quotation/vision_without_action_is_a_daydream-action/13772.html
- Krzyzewski Mike, http://en.wikipedia.org/wiki/Mike_Krzyzewski
- Ward, William Arthur, https://www.goodreads.com/quotes/115824-we-can-choose-to-throw-stones-to-stumble-on-them
- Knievel, Evel, http://en.wikipedia.org/wiki/Evel_Knievel
- Ware, Eugene, https://www.goodreads.com/quotes/18486-all-glory-comes-from-daring-to-begin
- Southwest Airlines, http://www.blogsouthwest.com/owning-it-during-spirit-week/
- Welch, Jack, http://www.iwise.com/24pC1
- Forster, E.M., https://www.goodreads.com/quotes/482803-one-person-with-passion-is-better-than-forty-people-merely
- Zig Ziglar quote http://thinkexist.com/quotation/people_often_say_that_motivation_doesn-t_last/145449.html

Does Your Team And Organization Practice

21st Century Leadership?

The 7 Key Attributes For Success

<u>Are You A:</u>

Servant Leader

Storyteller

Collaborator

Innovator

Daredevil

Adaptor

Global Citizen

Visit <u>www.StepBackFromTheBaggageClaim.com</u> or
<u>www.StepBackLeadership.com</u>
and begin the conversation with your team!
Speeches, workshops, and other resources available.

Jason Barger is

a dad, husband, friend, coffee drinker, Buckeye fan, and curious human. He is the globally celebrated creator of the *Step Back from the Baggage Claim* movement — highlighted by the New York Times, Kiplinger,

International Herald Tribune, and many other spots worldwide. As founder of Step Back Leadership Consulting LLC, Jason is a highly sought-after keynote speaker and also adds value to organizations through workshops, coaching, and consulting focused on leadership development, culture-shaping, service, and clarity of mission / vision.

Prior to taking off to sleep in airports and observe human behavior, Jason led 1,700 people to construct 125 houses internationally for families living in poverty. He is a graduate of Denison University, where he served as Captain of the men's basketball team, and then received certification from Georgetown University in Nonprofit Executive Management. In 2004, he was one of five people in Columbus, Ohio, to receive a Jefferson Award, a national award given to "ordinary people doing extraordinary things."

Today, Jason, his wife Amy, and their children, Will, Benton and Brooke, live in Columbus, Ohio.

To learn more, visit
StepBackFromTheBaggageClaim.com
or JasonVBarger.com or BookRemember.com
Follow on Twitter @StepBackBook or @JasonVBarger

Who Needs
To ReMember?

We All Need Reminders

Jason Barger's books are not meant to sit on shelves. They are meant to be shared. They are meant to begin conversations. They are meant to spread a positive spirit around the world.

Who in your life could benefit from thinking about the messages, questions and lessons in this book? Who are the individuals, teams or organizations who could benefit from intentional time to ReMember?

Dare to share.
Give it away to someone along your path!

BookRemember.com

(email info@BookRemember.com to purchase discounted bulk copies for your team or organization)

Learn about Jason's other books at
StepBackFromTheBaggageClaim.com